THE ART OF THE
IMPRESSIONISTS

THE ART OF THE
IMPRESSIONISTS

SCOTT REYBURN

SILVERDALE BOOKS

A QUANTUM BOOK

This edition published by Silverdale Books,
an imprint of Bookmart Ltd., in 2004

Bookmart Ltd.
Blaby Road
Wigston
Leicester
LE18 4SE

ISBN 1-84509-090-X

QUMAOI

Printed in Singapore by
Star Standard Industries (Pte) Ltd.

PICTURE CREDITS

CONTENTS

Claude MONET, Impression:
Sunrise, *1873, Paris, Musée*
Marmottan (now stolen).

INTRODUCTION

*I*mpressionism was, and is, a much-abused artistic term. It first appeared in Louis Leroy's mocking review of the *Première exposition* by the *Société anonyme coopérative d'artistes-peintres sculpteurs graveurs etc* which had opened at the Paris studios of the photographer Nadar on 15 April, 1874. The exhibition was the showpiece of an independent group of radical painters whose leading members included Monet, Renoir, Degas, Morisot, Pissarro, Sisley and Cézanne. Monet's *Impression: Sunrise* (1873, Paris, Musée Marmottan [now stolen]) bore the brunt of Leroy's rather laboured satire, and it is this work that evidently inspired the facetious, yet momentous, references to impressionist paintings. Leroy's article appeared in the satirical journal *Le Charivari* on 25 April, 1874; four days later 'Impressionism' was discussed more positively by Jules Castagnary in *Le Siècle*. Whether the artists liked it or not, the soubriquet 'Impressionism' had come into being and, for want of a better word to describe their shared aesthetic, it stuck. At a third exhibition given by the group in 1877, a placard announcing an *Exposition des impressionistes* was duly placed above the entrance to the galleries.

Now, over a century later, Impressionism has an almost talismatic allure for art historians, museum curators, fine art auctioneers, dealers, collectors, and the general public. No expression of Western artistic tradition is more popular – or more expensive – than an Impressionist painting. The magical term 'Impressionism' has recently been extended to artists, indeed whole schools, which have the most tenuous affiliations with the Parisian avant-garde of the 1870s.

Impressionism as a definable aesthetic is in danger of becoming as nebulous as the surface of a Monet lily pond.

What, then, is the archetypal Impressionist painting? What are its concerns and intentions? How can we distinguish between the Impressionist and the impressionistic? It is the aim of this brief survey to outline the principles that distinguish the epoch-making paintings of radical French artists during the latter half of the 19th century.

What has come to be known as the Impressionist 'revolution' was in many ways a more organic process of evolution, which was generated by a wide range of precursors. The desiccated institutions of the French Academic establishment had been a common enemy for independent-minded artists since the beginning of the 19th century, yet few had pursued and even fewer achieved the fusion of innovatory technique and subject matter so characteristic of Impressionism. By 1860 a retreat from modernism could even be detected in the *enfants terribles* of earlier 19th-century French painting. Eugène Delacroix (1798–1863), technically the most innovative of early 19th-century painters, had retreated to his ivory tower, repelled by a Paris populated with 'prostitutes and schemers', while the heroic, egotistical Realism of Gustave Courbet (1819–77) remained fixed in the artist's rural roots and was executed in the dark, bituminous media of a conformist Salon painter. As the industrialization and urbanization of France accelerated during the 1850s and '60s, it would be left to a younger generation of artists to find a new way of painting a new world.

PAINTERS
OF MODERN LIFE

*Edouard MANET, Execution of
the Emperor Maximilian, 1868,
Mannheim, Kunsthalle. The
Emperor Maximilian of Mexico was
shot by a nationalist firing squad in
Querétero on 19 June, 1867. The
Hapsburg archduke had accepted the
throne in 1864 at the instigation of
Napoleon III of France, but early in
1867 the French Emperor withdrew
all French troops from Mexico,
leaving Maximilian at the mercy of a
nationalist uprising led by Juárez.
Manet pointedly dresses the firing
squad in French uniforms in a
composition which owes much to
Goya's powerful scenes of war
atrocities.*

*I*n 1852 Louis Napoleon was proclaimed Napoleon III, Emperor of France, effectively bringing to a close the era of uncertainty and revolution following the downfall of Napoleon Bonaparte. The ensuing years of the Second Empire's 'elected dictatorship' (1852–70) saw an unprecedented expansion of the economy, offset by the skilful extension of the regime's authoritarian controls behind a facade of democratic toleration. Universal suffrage was restored – but the number of seats was reduced by two-thirds, and the elections were rigged to ensure a government majority. Even painting under the Second Empire was subject to its own forms of 'gerrymandering'.

The artistic *status quo* in mid 19th-century France was effectively controlled by one state-sponsored institution – the Académie des Beaux-Arts. Comprising 40 elected life members (14 painters, 8 sculptors, 8 architects, 4 engravers, 6 musical composers), the Academy was a self-perpetuating mediocracy which had successfully immunized itself against Romanticism, and which during the entire course of the century reluctantly admitted only three painters of the first rank into its fold – Baron Antoine Jean Gros (1771–1835), Jean Auguste Dominique Ingres (1780–1867) and Delacroix – all of whom had difficult relations with their fellow academicians.

Nevertheless it was the academicians who advised the government on matters of artistic policy, selected or rejected admissions for the Paris Salon, and judged the work of students of the state Ecole des Beaux-Arts in their attempts to win the prestigious Prix de Rome. The Academy saw itself as the protector of the nation's artistic well-being, its stance on 'progressive' tendencies epitomized by the comments of the Imperial Superintendent of Fine Arts, Count Nieuwerkerke, on Millet's rejected paintings at the Exposition Universelle of 1855: 'This is the painting of democrats, of those who don't change their linen, who want to put themselves over on men of the world; this art displeases and disgusts me.'

The great shop-window of French painting, sculpture and design was the Salon. The largest, most prestigious art exhibition in Europe, the Paris Salon was held every two years until 1833 and thereafter annually (except for a brief return to the biennial system from 1852–63). The Salon's original venue was the Louvre, but as the event expanded it was housed temporarily in the Tuileries (1849) and the Palais Royal (1850, 1852), before finding a more permanent home from 1857–97 in the Palais de l'Indus-trie, near the Champs Elysées. The Palais had been built for the Exposition Universelle of 1855, and it proved an appropriate enough venue for the almost production-line output of academic art during the Second Empire.

The Salon of 1785 had exhibited 197 paintings by 44 artists, all of whom were affiliated to the Academy. During the 1789 Revolution, Academician-only entry restrictions were removed and the Salon expanded accordingly, so that by 1857 it included a total of 2,715 paintings. Attendances were similarly prodigious – 518,892 people visited the 1876 Salon over its three-month duration (compared with the 3,500 over two months who visited what we now term the first Impressionist exhibition of 1874). An entrance fee was charged during the week, but admission was free on a Sunday and on a fine day 50,000 people could be expected to see the exhibits.

With the role of the independent dealer as yet limited, the Salon was one of the few means artists had of selling their work and gaining critical recognition. If a painting was accepted by the jury, the artist's address would be printed in the catalogue and contacts might be made with potential clients. If a painting was rejected, the letter *R* or *refusé* might be stamped on the stretcher, rendering it difficult to re-sell. The extent to which the Salon jury functioned as arbiters of middle-class taste was highlighted by the case of the landscape painter Johan Barthold Jongkind (1819–91) who sold a painting to a client who then demanded his money back when it was refused by the Salon.

The conservative tendencies of the admissions jury and the philistine tastes of the Second Empire's bourgeois audience inevitably generated a recognizable Salon style. *Phryne before the Areopagites* (1861, Hamburg, Kunsthalle) by Jean-Léon Gérôme (1824–1904) is representative of the idiom. An exotic, historical setting; a theatrical 'plot'; titillation for the voyeur (ironically reflected in the reactions of the Areopagites) combined with a morally edifying 'message'; a contrived verisimilitude – these were the typical ingredients of the Salon painter's brew.

....
Hyppolyte FLANDRIN, *Napoleon III, c.1860–61, Versailles, Musée National du Château. The Emperor's role in the transformation of 19th-century France is subtly advertised by a political pamphlet and a plan of Paris strategically placed on the table.*
....

C. MARAND, engraving of the
interior of the 1863 Salon.
Flandrin's portrait of Napoleon III
can be seen again in the lower centre
of the lefthand wall.

Notwithstanding the efforts of Courbet, Daumier, Millet *et al* to confront the Academic establishment, by 1860 it had become clear that painting was lagging behind literature in addressing the issues of the contemporary world. In 1857, *Les Fleurs du Mal* by the poet and critic Charles Baudelaire (1821–67) and *Madame Bovary* by Gustave Flaubert (1821–80) were both condemned as offensive to public morals, and as early as 1845, in his review of the Salon of that year, Baudelaire had exhorted artists to take the modern, urban world as their subject.

Baudelaire was the first critic to draw the crucial distinction between contemporary art and *modernité*. But at that time, significantly, he visualized the new painting as 'heroic' and 'epic' – exactly those qualities desired of the history painting that academic hierarchies regarded as pre-eminent.

A more mature combination of modern form and content was visualized in Baudelaire's famous essay, *The Painter of Modern Life*, published by *Le Figaro* in instalments from November to December 1863 (but written from November 1859 to December 1860). Using as a prototype the self-taught newspaper illustrator Constantin Guys (1802–92), Baudelaire enumerated the qualities required of the new artist. He is 'a man of the whole world', a man of the crowd, a philosopher, a dandy, a *flâneur* who observes and evokes 'bourgeois life and the pageant of fashion' in its glorious, transient entirety.

Guys was too old, and technically and imaginatively too limited an artist, to be able to extend Baudelaire's programme of *modernité*; a more formidable, if at times reluctant, ally would prove to be Edouard Manet (1832–83).

The son of a senior civil servant in the Ministry of Justice, Manet was ideally placed to take on the role of the bourgeois artist-as-dandy. In 1850, at the age of 18, he had joined the studio of Thomas Couture (1815–79), a history painter of independent status whose reputation had been made with the huge *Romans of the Decadence* (1847, Paris, Musée d'Orsay) that had been the sensation of the 1847 Salon. Manet's youthful arrogance may have dismissed Couture's *atelier* as 'a tomb', but it was here that over the next six years he gained a solid grounding in the academic painter's technical procedures.

The training at Couture's independent *atelier* broadly followed the practices of the state Ecole des Beaux-Arts, but with some important differences of emphasis. Drawing was the foundation of this training, starting from the 'flat' (ie engravings) before progressing to studies from casts and the live model. Drawn (or painted) studies after Masters in the Louvre were also encouraged. The student's own mastery of the painting medium required the coordination of preparatory techniques such as the *croquis* (a rough compositional sketch), the *esquisse* (a painted compositional sketch), and the *étude* (a painted or drawn

*A B O V E Jean-Léon GÉRÔME,
Phryne before the Areopagites,
1861, Hamburg, Kunsthalle. The
4th-century BC courtesan Phryne
appeared before the Athenian judicial
council (the Areopagus) on charges of
impiety.*

*L E F T Etienne CARJAT,
photograph of Charles Baudelaire.*

study of details). The composition finalized, the student could then prepare his *tableau* (a canvas intended for completion) which was first sealed with size, and then primed (traditionally with a lead-based paint). The student would then begin the *ébauche*, the broadly handled lay-in of lines and tonal underpainting. Dark masses were painted using thin solutions of red ochre and turpentine (known as 'sauce') applied with wide brushes or cloths; light masses were applied using *impasto*, a technique of applying paint heavily, which lends the academic nude its characteristic marble-like sheen. Next, at least six middle tones (*demi-teintes*) would be applied over the lights to form a link with the darks. These were not applied in layers, but in patches side-by-side as if working on a mosaic. As the work reached its latter stages, they would eventually be 'joined-up' to create a seamless transition of tone.

NADAR, *photograph of Edouard Manet. Taken c.1875, the photograph shows Manet in his early 40s.*

Couture, with his insistence on proportion, perspective and the 'classical' idealization of the figure was in some ways an old-fashioned figure, but in others he was remarkably forward-looking. He was unusual in emphasizing the expressive qualities of the *ébauche*, often leaving areas of this underpainting visible in the exhibited canvas (*The Decadence of the Romans* had been criticized for its 'unfinished' qualities). He would sometimes work 'wet-in-wet', applying paint on top of a still tacky *ébauche*. He encouraged his students to preserve the 'freshness' and 'purity' of colours, and 'to look at the model only to render your first impression'. But perhaps most important of all, his unpopularity with the Academy infected his students, such as Manet, with a refreshing independence of mind. Both Couture the conformist and Couture

the non-conformist were to be reflected in Manet's mature work of the 1860s.

In 1861 Manet tasted early success at the Salon with *The Spanish Singer* (1860, New York, Metropolitan Museum of Art) which was awarded 'an honourable mention' (thanks probably to the intervention of Delacroix). It was one of several Spanish costume pieces executed in the early 1860s which perhaps owed as much to the current Parisian vogue for things Spanish – stimulated by Napoleon III's recent marriage to Eugénie de Montijo – as to Manet's reverence for the painterliness of Spanish Old Masters such as Diego Rodriguez de Silva y Velasquez (1599–1660), whom he called 'the painter of painters'.

1861 was also the year in which Baudelaire met Manet for the first time. The poet immediately recognized his brilliance and 'feeble character'. However, the following year – perhaps through the direct influence of Baudelaire – Manet's painting began to address more overtly 'modern' subject matter, and in an article published in the autumn of 1862 Baudelaire championed the young artist for his 'decided taste for modern truth'.

But modernity was more than a mere artistic talking-point in the Paris of the 1860s. Under the ruthless prefecture of Baron Haussmann, the very fabric of the city itself was being transformed. The delapidated, medieval, working-class *quartiers* of central Paris, the traditional breeding grounds of revolution, were swept away and their inhabitants resettled in the undeveloped suburbs. In their place rose elegant new apartment blocks, department stores, cafés, new open spaces, and new, broad, straight, boulevards which provided both a more pleasant environment for the pedestrian and, in the event of future insurrection, a wider field of fire for government troops.

By 1870, after 17 years of 'Haussmannization' at a total cost of 2.5 billion francs (including 80 million on sewerage alone), one-fifth of all the streets of central Paris had been rebuilt, displacing some 350,000 citizens. Those workers who had not been forced out of the centre of Paris by demolition were instead forced out by inflationary rents, which doubled between 1851 and 1857. By the eve of the Franco-Prussian war, Haussmann's vision of 'disembowelling the old Paris, the *quartier* of uprisings and barricades' had been substantially realized.

The freshly constructed boulevards became a playground for the bourgeois self-made men, the manufacturers, bankers, and property speculators who had

....
*Thomas COUTURE, Romans of
the Decadence, 1847, Paris,
Musée d'Orsay. This vast, eclectic
painting – measuring over 15¹/₄ ×
24³/₄ft/4.66 × 7.55m – was the
sensation of the 1847 Salon.*
....

profited out of the Second Empire's economic boom. Between 1851 and 1869 France's industrial production increased by 50 per cent, her exports by 150 per cent. Between 1852 and 1860 railway investment increased by 500 per cent, a modern banking system was developed and huge profits were made out of the redevelopment of Paris. One commentator in 1867 described the new Rue de Rivoli (completed in 1858 after uprooting 12,000 people):

The Rue de Rivoli is a symbol; a new street, wide, long, cold, frequented by men as well dressed, affected, and cold as the street itself. (T. J. Clarke, *The Painting of Modern Life*, London, 1985.)

This is the New Paris evoked by Manet in *La Musique aux Tuileries (Music in the Tuileries Gardens*, 1862, London, National Gallery), his first painting of modern urban life. Executed probably in 1862, the composition portrays a gallery of contemporary artistic and social luminaries gathered at one of the fashionable outdoor concerts held twice-weekly in the Tuileries Gardens. Manet himself, the elegant, detached *flâneur*, can be seen on the extreme left.

As with all Manet's most ambitious paintings of the 1860s, it is a tense fusion of tradition and modernity.

The informal figure grouping has roots in similar outdoor group portraits of the 18th century, by artists such as Philibert-Louis Debucourt (1755–1832), whose aquatint of *La Promenade Publique* (1792, British Museum) would certainly have been known to Manet. The specific positioning of the figures in Manet's work derives from a Spanish painting of Cavaliers in the Louvre, which at that time was attributed to Velasquez, and which Manet both painted and etched. Manet draws a witty analogy between himself and Velasquez as 'court' painters by placing himself in the same position as a supposed self-portrait of Velasquez in the Louvre composition.

As well as traditional sources, the painting also draws on a wide range of more ephemeral, contemporary, visual material such as lithographs, newspaper illustrations and photographs. The impact of photography may be of central importance. The painting's rejection of half-tones, the strong frontal

*Jean-Léon GÉRÔME, The Greek
Slave, c.1869, Boston, Museum of
Fine Arts.*

MARTIAL, engraving, c.1860, of demolition and excavation in preparation for the construction of the new Boulevard Malesherbes, Paris.

Engraving of the inauguration of the Boulevard Malesherbes, 13 August, 1861.

lighting, the summarily painted 'flat' theatrical backdrop, the figure's frozen poses gazing at the observer, their ebb and flow in and out of focus – all seem to suggest a crowd caught in the momentary glare of a studio photographer's flash.

The execution of *La Musique aux Tuileries* is as radical as its composition. Manet shifts the points of emphasis of the Salon painter's technical procedures: instead of gradated tones being meticulously laid in over dark priming to produce a smooth surface, Manet accentuates the unfinished qualities of the *ébauche*, applies the paint with the freedom of an *esquisse*, and leaves the surface of the picture loose and textured.

The dark backdrop is thinly laid in with a palette knife over a predominantly unprimed white canvas. The lights and darks of the figures below are more thickly applied with the brush and, particularly in the drapery of the seated ladies on the left, incisively worked wet-in-wet. Instead of devising subtle transitions of tone, Manet employs stark tonal clashes liberally using black (much loved by the Spanish Masters, but abominated by the Salon); these tonal 'clashes' are in turn set off by vivid highlights of local colour.

This painterly freedom owes much to Manet's use of poppy oil as a medium rather than the more traditional binder, linseed. Pigments ground in poppy oil take longer to dry and have a 'creamier' consistency, which retains the imprint of the brush and palette knife.

Strictly speaking, this painting cannot claim to be the first Impressionist painting. It was, after all, painted in a studio (from studies drawn in the Tuileries) over a considerable length of time. But it can claim to be the first truly *modern* painting of the 19th century. True to the vision of a human eye scanning a crowd, *La Musique aux Tuileries* appears to have no 'composition', no centre of focus, and, most provocative of all, who, or what, is that grey smudge in the middle of the picture to the left of Manet's brother Eugène? No painting of the time comes closer to the Baudelarian ideal of *modernité*:

The crowd is his element, as the air is that of birds and water fishes. His passion and his profession are to become one flesh with the crowd. For the perfect *flâneur*, for the passionate spectator, it is an immense joy to set up house in the heart of the multitude, amid the ebb and flow of movement, in the midst of the fugitive and the infinite. (Charles Baudelaire, *The Painter of Modern Life*, [trans. Jonathan Mayne], London, 1964.)

When the painting was exhibited in February 1863 at the Galerie Louis Martinet, it was greeted by a predictably hostile reception. The novelist and critic Emile Zola recounted that an outraged art lover even threatened violence if *La Musique aux Tuileries* remained in the gallery a moment longer.

Controversy also clouded Manet's relations with the Salon of that year. The jury of 1863 had been

Edouard MANET, Music in the
Tuileries Gardens, *c.1862*,
London, National Gallery.

exceptionally severe, particularly on younger artists, accepting only 2,217 of the 5,000 works submitted. Manet had entered three paintings – *Le Déjeuner sur l'Herbe* (1863, Paris, Musée d'Orsay), *Young Man in Majo Costume* (1863, New York, Metropolitan Museum), *Mlle V. in the Costume of an Espada* (1862, New York, Metropolitan Museum of Art) – all of which were rejected. Manet and the illustrator Gustave Doré (1832–83) headed a seemingly fruitless deputation on behalf of the rejected artists to the Minister of Fine Arts, Count Walewski. But on 24 April a notice appeared in *Le Moniteur Universel* announcing that the Emperor had heard of their grievances. He wished the public to judge for themselves and therefore had arranged for a simultaneous exhibition of these rejected works in a gallery adjoining the Palais d'Industrie.

The major talking point of this exhibition, now known as the Salon des Refusés, was Manet's *Le Déjeuner sur l'Herbe*. This painting derives its mood from Giorgione's *Concert champêtre* in the Louvre (c. 1510), and its specific disposition of figures from Marcantonio Raimondi's engraving after Raphael of *The Judgement of Paris*. These Renaissance allusions are updated by a wilful dislocation of the laws of perspective, disconcerting anomalies of scale, tension between exterior setting and studio lighting, but above all by the presence of an 'unartistically' rendered nude woman drying herself in the open air beside two fashionably dressed men. The Emperor described the subject as 'immodest', and the English critic Philip Hamerton summed up the unease generated by Manet's treatment of the nude which 'whenever painted by vulgar men, is inevitably indecent'.

The public and critical outrage generated by Manet's *modernité* reached a hysterical crescendo with the reception of *Olympia* (1863, Paris, Musée d'Orsay) at the 1865 Salon. Hung beneath Manet's other Salon entry, *The Mocking of Christ* (1865, Chicago, Art Institute), the *Olympia* (a common name for a prostitute) was accompanied by a catalogue entry with verses by the writer and sculptor Zachérie Astruc. They removed any doubt that the spectator might have had concerning the nature of the subject:

When, weary of dreaming, Olympia wakes,
Spring enters in the arms of a gentle black messenger;
it is the slave, like the amorous night,
who comes to make the day bloom, delicious to see;
the august young girl in whom the fire burns.
(T. J. Clarke, *The Painting of Modern Life*, London, 1985.)

The Salon opened in early May to 'laughter, mockery and catcalls'.

Courbet dismissed the figure as 'a playing card', and most critics (but, it should be stressed, not all) took a hostile stance on both the subject and technique of *Olympia*: 'Art which has sunk so low is not worthy even of censure' (Paul de Saint Victor) . . . 'a sort of female gorilla, a grotesque in Indian rubber outlined in black' (Amédée Cantaloube, *Le Grand Journal*) . . . 'like a corpse on the counters of the morgue, this Olympia from the Rue Mouffetard, dead of yellow fever and already arrived at an advanced state of decomposition' (Victor Fournel).

Towards the end of May, in response to the controversy, the authorities re-hung the *Olympia* and the *Christ* in less conspicuous positions.

As in *Le Déjeuner sur l'Herbe*, the starting point of the *Olympia* was a hallowed High Renaissance masterpiece – Titian's *Venus of Urbino* (1538, Florence, Uffizi), which Manet had copied probably during his second visit to Italy in 1856. That this allusion was regarded as almost 'sacrilegious' indicates that Titian's nude must have lost most of the erotic charge that had made it unacceptable to its original patron, Emperor Charles V. What 19th-century observers of Titian tended to forget was that Venice in the 16th century,

like Paris in the 19th, was a city with a large courtesan population. At that time it was estimated that Venice had a population of around 15,000 prostitutes, whereas that of Paris in the 1850s was conservatively estimated at around 34,000. Both Titian's *Venus of Urbino,* and Manet's *Olympia* are paintings of prostitutes, and both take their place in the established European tradition of the 'boudoir' picture. Another example, with correspondingly compromising overtones for the observer, is Velasquez' *Rokeby Venus* (c. 1648–51, London, National Gallery).

What 1865 Salon audiences found so outrageous and threatening about the *Olympia* was not so much that she was a prostitute – images of the fallen woman,

the libertine, were not uncommon, even in Salon painting (Gérôme's *Phryne before the Areopagites* for example) – but that she was depicted as an *individualized* prostitute of that day. Mythologized, generalized, and anaesthetized nudes such as Félix-Henri Giacometti's *Rape of Amymona* (1865, Lisle-sur-Tarn, Musée Raymond) were bought by the State that year, but a naked woman one might be meeting that afternoon was a different matter. The male observer was further compromised by Olympia confronting him as an individual, implicating him as the client. The sensuality of the image is further enforced by Manet's succulent handling of paint, playing off the warm tints of living flesh against the subtly modulated whites of the sheet and the grey of the shawl; the strategic placement of the brilliantly foreshortened left hand; and by the more obvious symbols of lasciviousness, such as the cat (a typically Baudelarian image).

After such a direct confrontation of bourgeois hypocrisy, it was not surprising that Manet found it

....
BERTALL, Manette, *or* The
Cabinetmaker's Wife, by Manet,
wood engraving, published in Le
Journal Amusant, *27 May, 1865.
The caption describes how 'The great
colourist has chosen the moment when
the lady is about to take a much-
needed bath'. Manet's deployment of
black shadows was one of the main
targets for satirists of Olympia.*
....

difficult to shake off the label of being the painter of
Olympia. During the height of the controversy over
what was arguably Manet's greatest painting, the
painter wrote in desperation to Baudelaire in Brussels
complaining that 'they're raining insults on me, I've
never been led such a dance'. Baudelaire was unsym-
pathetic.

Baudelaire had gone to Brussels in 1864, despe-
rately hoping to supplement his meagre resources by
lecturing. The expedition was an utter failure; he was
struck by general paralysis in March 1866, and then
brought back to Paris the following year where he
died on 31 August, 1867. Two days later Manet
attended Baudelaire's funeral in the Cimetière Montparnasse, an event full of ominous *correspondances*
between man and nature which the poet would have
relished. The day was dark and stormy – the eulogy
was interrupted by rain – and in *The Burial* (c. 1867,
New York, Metropolitan Museum) this is evoked by
Manet with an emotional power fuelled by the mood
of Baudelaire's poetry, and reflections from a recent
visit to Spain where he had seen Velasquez' and El
Greco's brooding landscapes.

Manet in the 1860s was a sphinx-like figure, on the
one hand outrageously confronting the Salon and its
audience, on the other craving its acceptance. Indeed,
he was to say (and prove) later to the Impressionists
that the Salon is 'the true field of battle – it is there

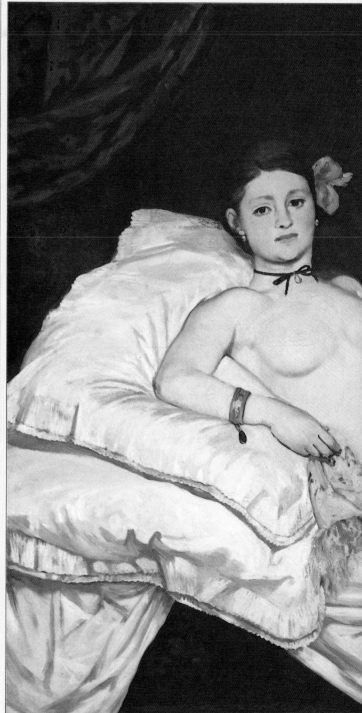

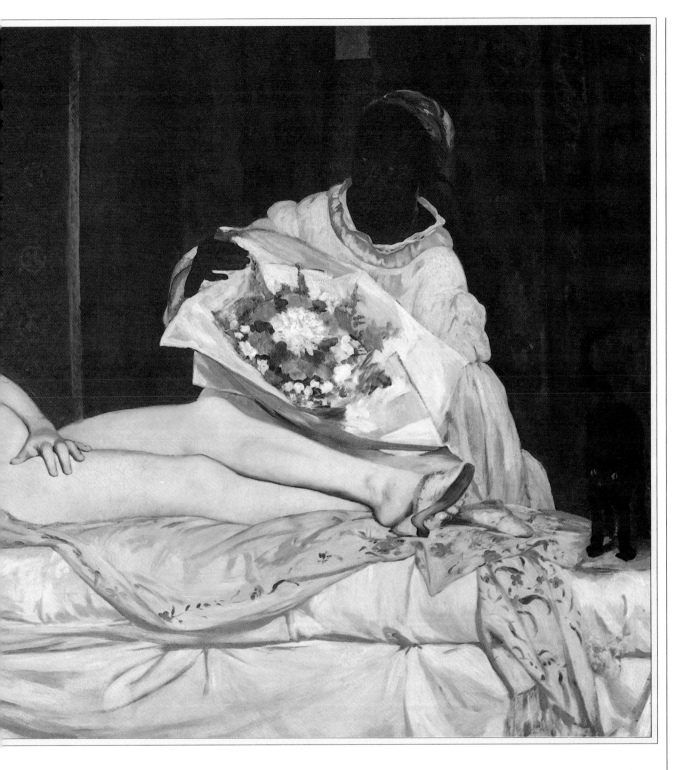

Edouard MANET, Olympia, 1863,
Paris, Musée d'Orsay.

ABOVE Edouard MANET,
The Burial, *c.1867, New
York, Metropolitan Museum
of Art. This unfinished
painting (once owned by
Pissarro) in all probability
depicts Baudelaire's funeral
cortège. The poet was buried
in the Cimitière
Montparnasse in stormy
weather on 2 September,
1867, and in the distance to
the north can be seen the
domes of the Panthéon and
the Val de Grâce.*

....

LEFT TITIAN, Venus of
Urbino, *1538, Florence,
Uffizi. Manet copied this
famous Titian masterpiece
probably during a second visit
to Italy in 1856.*

....

one must measure oneself'. Contemporary and subsequent observers have been baffled by his numerous references to Old Masters in his paintings, often interpreting this as mere poverty of imagination. Or were these often blatant references deliberately designed to set up a creative tension between tradition and modernity?

Apart from provocation, Manet's allusions to the Old Masters might well have been an attempt to set up an 'eternal' beauty, side by side with the 'temporal' beauty of the Second Empire's prostitutes and patent-leather boots. It is perhaps dangerous to stress ideological links between painters and writers. But in Manet's pictures painted after Baudelaire's death in 1867 there is a noticeable slackening of provocative subject matter and art historical references (with the great exception of *The Execution of the Emperor Maximilian*, the first of several versions of which was started in late 1867). Manet's later paintings begin to explore the possibilities offered by Impressionism. But if Manet had chosen to look back at the 1860s, he, as much as Baudelaire, deserved Victor Hugo's tribute to *Les Fleurs du Mal:* 'vous avez crée un frisson nouveau'.

In contrast to the creative tensions of Manet's painting in the 1860s, the art of Edgar Degas (1843–1917) unifies tradition and modernity. If Manet was the 17th-century Spanish painter of modern Paris, Degas was its Renaissance Florentine, a notion voiced by Degas himself in his notebooks – 'Oh Giotto! Let me see Paris, and you Paris, let me see Giotto!'

Degas, like Manet, came from an affluent Parisian background. His father Auguste de Gas (the artist contracted the surname) was an aesthetically minded banker with ramified family connections throughout France, Italy and America. The painter was fortunate in having a father more interested in culture than commerce, who introduced him at an early age to major collections and collectors of art.

In 1855, at the age of 21, Degas is reputed to have been instrumental in persuading his father's friend, the collector Edouard Valpincon, to lend Ingres' *Bather* (1808, Paris, Louvre), the great icon of the French 19th-century classical tradition, to the artist's display in the Exposition Universelle of that year. In return, Valpincon arranged for Degas to meet the aged Ingres, who gave the younger artist some advice he was not to forget: 'Draw lines, young man, many lines; from memory or from nature, it is in this that you will become a good artist.'

Edgar DEGAS, Self Portrait in formal dress, *c.1854, Paris, Louvre. Using a pose reminiscent of a portrait by his mentor Ingres, this is one of the earliest of 11 self-portraits painted by Degas between 1854 and 1858.*

Degas studied painting briefly at the Ecole des Beaux-Arts, supplemented by assiduous copying of the Masters in the Louvre (where he was to meet Manet in 1862). But the most important formative period of Degas' artistic education occurred in Italy during two extended study tours undertaken from 1856 to 1859.

Much of Degas' early work consists of portraits of himself and his immediate family. But on his return to Paris in 1859, having installed himself with a private income in a studio in the Rue Madame, he applied himself for the next five years to a series of 'heroic', large-scale, history paintings with which he hoped to make his reputation at the Salon. In later life Degas could be dismissive about a work such as *The Young Spartans Exercising* (begun c.1860, London, National Gallery), but the painting was always hung in a prominent position in his house, and was fitfully reworked over a period of 20 years (in common with a number of his earlier works) before being exhibited in the

fifth Impressionist exhibition of 1880. Its methodical, studio-based execution is representative of Degas' creative processes throughout the 1860s.

The Young Spartans Exercising – a subject from Plutarch's *Life of Lycurgus*, redolent of Degas' awkward relations with the opposite sex – evolved through a succession of numerous notebook studies and separate drawings, four oil sketches and two large-scale canvases (in which the prominent motif of a temple was abandoned). In its painstaking and refined composition and choice of classical subject matter the painting follows the academic traditions of Ingres and his school. Indeed, the frieze-like arrangement of figures in opposed groups and the logical spatial progression from foreground, through middle ground, to background can be compared to Ingres' *Achilles Receiving the Ambassadors of Agamemnon* (1801, Paris, Ecole des Beaux-Arts). But looking beyond these external associations, one can see that Degas fundamentally rejected the idealization of academic painting. Instead, his adolescents are realized not as the perfectly modelled inhabitants of a studio-lit, classical never-never land, but as the tough, wiry *gamins* of the Paris streets standing out in the open air.

After the success of the mysterious *War Scene from the Middle Ages*, (1865, Paris, Musée d'Orsay), which was accepted for the Salon of 1865, the uneasy alliance between Degas' innovation and academic history painting is resolved by the creation of his own 'modern' history paintings. A catalyst for this change of direction was Degas' exposure to the circle of Manet, among which Emile Zola was a conspicuous member.

Zola's novel *Thérèse Raquin* has been convincingly identified as the source for Degas' powerful and enigmatic *Interior* (1868–9, Philadelphia, Private Collection, Henry P. Mcilhenny). Once again the painter takes up the theme of men and women unable to 'connect', but now in a contemporary setting. *Thérèse Raquin*, a grim, uncompromisingly naturalistic tale of adultery, murder and revenge, created a scandal on its publication in 1867 and was denounced by critics as pornography. Degas' painting focusses on the psychological climax of the book – the loveless wedding night of Thérèse and her lover, Laurent, two years after they had murdered her first husband, Camille:

Laurent carefully shut the door behind him, then stood leaning against it for a moment looking into the room, ill at ease and embarrassed . . . A good fire was blazing in the hearth, setting great patches of golden light dancing on the ceiling and walls, illuminating the whole room with a bright and flickering radiance against which the lamp on the table seemed but a feeble glimmer . . . Thérèse was sitting on a low chair to the right of the fireplace, her chin cupped in her hand, staring at the flames. She did not look round when Laurent came in. Her lacy petticoat and bodice showed up dead white in the light of the blazing fire. The bodice was slipping down and part of her shoulder emerged pink, half hidden by a tress of her black hair . . . They looked at each other with no desire but only timid awkwardness, irked at staying silent and cold . . . Each of them was facing the terrifying fact that their passion was dead, that by killing Camille they had killed their own desire . . . Such was their wedding night (Zola, *Thérèse Raquin*, Penguin, London, 1962).

Sexual tension and emotional alienation are intensified in the painting by the eerie light playing

....
ABOVE Edgar DEGAS, The Young Spartans Exercising, *begun c.1860, London, National Gallery.*
....

OPPOSITE PAGE
Edgar DEGAS, The Bellelli Family, *c. 1858–60, Paris, Musée d'Orsay.*
....

over Thérèse's back and the wide-angle perspective, in which the floorboards seem to be slipping away from under Laurent's feet. Particularly fond of the picture, Degas refused to identify its subject and referred to it as 'my genre painting'.

The quasi-scientific naturalism of Zola's fiction also seems to have been influential on Degas' portraits during this period. Earlier works such as the virtuoso *Bellelli Family* (c.1858–60, Paris, Musée d'Orsay) had updated the formulae of Ingres' portraits – the

frieze-like disposition of figures and use of a mirror to expand pictorial space are Ingres' trademarks. But by the later 1860s Degas began to evolve a new approach to portraiture which was recorded in his notebooks:

Make portraits of people in typical, familiar poses, being sure above all to give their faces the same kind of expression as their bodies. Thus if laughter typifies an individual, make her laugh. There are, of course, feelings which one cannot convey, out of propriety, as portraits are not intended for us painters alone. How many delicate nuances to put in . . .
Make of the *tête d'expression* a study of modern feeling.' [*Degas by Himself*, MacDonald/Orbis, 1987].

One of Degas' first, most compelling, studies of 'modern feeling' is his portrait of *Victoria Dubourg* (1866, Toledo, Museum of Art), a painting remarkable for its assymetric composition boldly exposing a large area of blank wall, and originality of pose. Victoria Dubourg was a member of the Manet circle who was to later marry the handsome painter Fantin-Latour, much to the pique of Berthe Morisot. Her intelligence and strength of personality are powerfully conveyed by the simple, direct pose in which she leans forward attentively, as if listening, a half-smile playing across her lips. This directness is enforced by the painting's colour which is subdued in range but vibrant in hue – a result of Degas drying out the oil from his pigments on blotting paper and applying them to the canvas in thin washes saturated with turpentine.

By the end of the 1860s Degas and Manet had thus achieved modernity of both form and content in their paintings of the contemporary urban scene. During the next decade the two artists were to confront in very different ways the possibilities and problems of developing this new idiom.

CHAPTER TWO

THE BREATH
OF FRESH AIR

Claude MONET, Women in the
Garden, *1866, Paris, Musée
d'Orsay.*

*I*n the early 19th century the French Academy still adhered to a hierarchy of painting types which stretched back to the Academy's establishment in the 1640s. Unquestioned at the summit of this hierarchy was history painting; below it lay 'historical' landscapes, portraits, and paintings of religious subjects; and at the lowest level, genre scenes (ie of everyday life), 'rural' landscapes, and still life.

The prestige of historical landscape in France was largely based on the achievements of the French 17th-century painters Nicolas Poussin (1594–1665) and Claude Lorraine (1600–82), both of whom lived and worked in Italy. It was their classicizing vision of the landscape that shaped much of European landscape painting from the late 17th century, through the 18th century, to the 19th century and beyond.

In Poussin's *Landscape with the Funeral of Phocion* (1648, Cardiff, National Museum of Wales) the observer's eye is led through the landscape by a number of compositional devices: a dark foreground and a large overhanging tree push the eye into the middle distance (devices known as *repoussoirs*); the eye then zig-zags through a series of intersecting wings (*coulisses*) before reaching the distant hills. The sense of depth in the painting is also achieved by aerial perspective, combining tonal (from dark to light) and colouristic (brown to green to blue) recessions. The whole is governed by a timeless geometry which enhances the *gravitas* of the subject itself.

Almost two centuries later, the French Academy still regarded Poussin's and Claude's conception of the historical landscape as the most noble way of visualizing the landscape. Indeed, in 1817 its morally edifying, ennobling effects resulted in the inauguration of a historical landscape category in the Prix de Rome, the five-year old scholarship at the French Academy in Rome which was the ultimate goal of any academically oriented student. The aims of the historical landscape were outlined by J.B. Deperthes in *Théorie du Paysage* published in Paris in 1818:

The art of composing scenery from a selection of the most beautiful and the most noble that nature produces, and of introducing into it persons whose actions, whether they recall an historical act or present an imaginary subject, are able to arouse the keenest interest of the spectator, to inspire his noblest feelings and give wings to his imagination. (Albert Boime, *The Academy and French Painting in the 19th century*, London, 1971.

LEFT *Nicolas POUSSIN,*
Landscape with Funeral of
Phocion, *1648, Cardiff, National
Museum of Wales, Collection of the
Earl of Plymouth.*

ABOVE *Pierre-Henri de
VALENCIENNES, View of Rome,
c.1780, Paris, Louvre. An otherwise
orthodox historical landscape painter,
Valenciennes studied in Italy where he
executed these open-air oil studies.*

The other, less elevated, form of landscape paint-ing sanctioned by the Academy was the 'rural' land-scape whose aims were, according to J. B. Deperthes, 'To represent faithfully an expanse of country with the part of the sky which dominates it, and seen in the light that falls on it at the very moment when the painter sets out to capture its appearance.' (Ibid).

At first this more naturalistic approach to land-scape might seem to anticipate Impressionism, but it is in fact derived from the well-worn theories of 17th-century Dutch landscape painting. Nevertheless, it was the rural landscape tradition, with its more flexi-ble concentration on *observed* nature, that would be the basis for the most progressive trends in the 19th-century French landscape painting culminating, ulti-mately, in Impressionism.

As early as the late 18th century, a 'classical' land-scape painter such as Pierre-Henri de Valenciennes (1750–1819) criticized history painters for being the least capable of landscape painting because so few of them painted in the open air, and even fewer had painted a living model in sunlight. In the open air Valenciennes produced some remarkably fresh oil-on-paper *études* of the Italian landscape. He went even further by suggesting that they 'paint the same view at different times of day, so as to observe the modification of form under the action of light'. How-ever, he regarded these rapidly executed sketches as mere notations of the effects of light and atmosphere on scenery, and they bore little relation to his finished historical landscapes. Valenciennes' paradox, at least for 20th-century observers, is that he sketched in the rural tradition in preparation for his highly finished historical landscapes.

This gulf between sketch and finished painting was significantly reduced by J-B. Camille Corot (1796–1875), the most successful French landscape painter of the earlier 19th century. Corot's open-air studies made during his travels in Italy in the 1820s and '30s have remarkable similarities to Valenciennes' treatment of the same subject. But throughout his long career Corot respected the distinction between the open-air *étude* and the finished *tableau*. The one exception was the open-air study of *The Coliseum seen from the Farnese Gardens*, painted in Italy in 1826 and exhibited at the more relaxed post-Revolutionary Salon of 1849. Corot nonetheless felt compelled to give the study a more finished appearance by altering the trees and bushes on the right. What allowed him to exhibit a study at the Salon was that, like so many of his open-air studies, *The Coliseum* was even in its untouched state composed with the calculated structure of a finished painting.

It is Corot who forms the link between the 18th- and 19th-century French landscape traditions. In 1897, when Monet was looking through an important collection of Impressionist and other 19th-century paintings, he was moved to comment: 'There is only one person here, that's Corot: we others are nothing compared to him.' Yet Corot's relations with the Impressionists were double-edged. He supported and encouraged Pissarro, Sisley and Berthe Morisot, he advocated dispensing with 'finish' once the general effect had been achieved, and he subscribed to the credo that 'the artist should submit to the first impression'. Yet he discouraged Cézanne's friend Antoine Guillaumet from participating in the first Impressionist exhibition, saying: 'My dear Antoine, you have done very well to escape from that gang.'

Meanwhile, elsewhere in Europe the cult of 'truth to nature' had been less restricted by academic hierarchies. In England, the *plein-air* topographical watercolour had been a national speciality of both professional and amateur artists since the second half of the 18th century; and the Romantically inspired 'natural' landscape had reached its most monumental expression in the great 'six-foot' canvases of John Constable (1776–1837).

Constable used precisely the same technical procedures as a French academic landscape painter – drawings, oil studies of individual motifs, and compositional sketches – but what distinguished him from his French contemporaries was his analytical sensitivity to nature. *The Haywain* (1821, London, National Gallery), which so vividly evokes nature's shifting moods, created a sensation when exhibited at the 1824 Paris Salon (where it won a Gold Medal). After

Collapsible tin tubes of oil paint were perfected between 1841–43 by the London-based American artist John Goffe Rand. These rival Winsor and Newton tubes dating from c.1841–2 were among the first to be manufactured, but use stoppers rather than Rand's suggested screw caps which soon became standard.

seeing it at the Salon, Delacroix unwittingly wrote in his notebook of *The Haywain's* Impressionistic qualities: 'Constable says that the superiority of the green in his fields derives from the fact that it is made up of a multitude of different greens. The reason why the greenery of most landscapists lacks intensity and life is that they usually treat it in one single tint.' (John House, Monet: *Nature into Art*, Yale, 1986).

The Haywain had in fact been painted in Constable's London studio using open-air oil studies made some five years previously. Nearly all Constable's

....
John CONSTABLE, The
Haywain *(detail), 1821, London,*
National Gallery.
....

ABOVE *J.-B. Camille COROT*, The
Coliseum seen from the Farnese
Gardens, *1826, Paris, Louvre.*

BELOW *Pig's bladders had been the
traditional method for the open-air oil
painter to transport his colours. These
were sealed with ivory stoppers which
would not alter the chemical state of
the pigment, but once opened the
paint tended to deteriorate rapidly.*

major works were produced in the studio and he exhibited only two large-scale oil paintings which had
been executed entirely in the open-air – *Boat Building
near Flatford Mill* (1815) and *Water-Meadows near Salis-
bury* (1829/30), both London, Victoria and Albert
Museum). The latter was rejected by the Royal Academy in 1830 as a 'nasty green thing'.

For an early 19th-century painter such as Constable,
working from nature on a large scale in oil with its
slow drying times and bulky equipment, posed severe
logistical problems. Until the invention of collapsible
tin tubes in the 1840s, paint had to be bought in pig's
bladders sealed with ivory, and tended to deteriorate
rapidly once opened. Then there was always the
problem of changing weather. The problems facing
even the most determined open-air painters are
amusingly described by F. Henriet. Daubigny's
Villerville-sur-Mer (1864, The Hague, Mesdag
Museum), exhibited in the Salon of 1864, was among
the earliest large-scale landscapes to be painted entirely in the open air, apparently with some difficulty,
vulnerable as the canvas was to both the elements and
the inquisitiveness of the local inhabitants (both man
and beast).

Perhaps the most tenacious open-air painter
before Monet, Charles-Francois Daubigny (1817–78)

was also notable for using a boat as a floating studio (an idea later taken up by Monet). Daubigny's *botin* was launched in 1857, and he used it to explore the Seine and the Oise, recording his impressions in numerous small oil paintings. Daubigny was only one of a number of painters in France attempting to create a more natural depiction of landscape. The geographical focus of this movement was the forest of Fontainebleau, some 40 miles (64km) south-east of Paris, where, in the villages of Barbizon and Chailly, artists such as Corot, Narcisse Diaz (1808–76), Constant Troyon (1810–65), and Théodore Rousseau (1812–67) sketched the dense woodland. 'Barbizon' painting (as it came to be known) is a remarkably coherent style characterized by an essentially romantic view of nature in which tangled trees rise out of the dark, sodden earth to be silhouetted against lowering skies. This gloominess of vision tends to be intensified technically by the use of dark grounds and bituminous blacks for the shadows; much sketching was done in the open air, but the *tableau* was usually completed in the studio.

The naturalism of the Barbizon School landscapists was also taken up by French marine painters. One of the most notable of these painters was the Norman artist Eugène Boudin (1824–98), who, after 1851, gave up running a framemaker's shop in Le Havre to devote himself full time to painting. A determined practitioner of open-air painting, Boudin specialized in small, breezy scenes of the Normandy coast inhabited by the Parisian well-to-do on seaside excursions. In fact Boudin worked far more in the studio than was once believed – particularly for his larger canvases – but his influence on the young Monet, almost converting him to open-air painting, was an important catalyst for the development of Impressionism.

Claude Monet (1840–1926) was born in Paris, but in 1845, at the age of five, moved with his family to Sainte-Adresse, a suburb of Le Havre. Monet's father ran a wholesale grocery business in partnership with his brother-in-law, and the younger Monet grew up in an environment with few, if any, cultural pretensions. However, after his mother died in 1857 Monet's artistic interests were encouraged by an aunt, Marie-Jeanne Lecadre. While still a teenager he exhibited a precocious gift for caricature. One of these was noticed by Boudin in the window of the frame

....
A B O V E Charles-Francois DAUBIGNY, Riverbank, Herd Drinking, 1859, New York, The Brooklyn Museum. A composition probably executed, at least in part, from Daubigny's floating studio (botin) in which he explored the rivers of France.
....

shop he used to run. The two artists met, and after a certain amount of cajoling Boudin persuaded Monet to accompany him sketching the scenery around Le Havre. As Monet later said, 'Boudin, with untiring kindness, undertook my education. My eyes were finally opened and I really understood nature; I learned at the same time to love it.'

By 1858 Monet had exhibited a painting at an exhibition in Le Havre. The following year, using the income from his caricatures, he stayed in Paris. There he visited the 1859 Exposition Universelle, where he admired the works of Corot, Daubigny and the Barbizon school, but lamented in a letter to Boudin that there wasn't a single marine painting that he felt was passable.

In 1861 Monet was called up for military service. He chose to serve with the Chasseurs d'Afrique in Algeria but was invalided out after a year. As with the other great French colourist of the 19th century, Eugéne Delacroix (who visited Morocco in 1832), the experience of the clear North African light intensified Monet's perceptions. A year later in 1862, probably subsidized by his aunt, Monet returned to Paris where he studied for two years in the studio of Charles Gleyre, a relatively broad-minded, if uninspiring, Swiss-born Salon painter. In later life Monet was dismissive about this period of academic training, maintaining that its real importance lay in the contact he made with Pierre Auguste Renoir (1841–1919), Alfred Sisley (1839–99) and Frédéric Bazille (1841–71), who were all fellow pupils in Gleyre's studio.

Monet's pre-Impressionist works up to 1865 fall into two main groups. The first is his Normandy marine scenes, derived from the example of Boudin and increasingly influenced by the luminous open-air watercolours of the Dutch-born painter Jongkind, whom he had met at Le Havre in 1862. The other group is of landscape paintings, inspired by the Barbizon group and executed from studies and sketches made in the forest of Fontainebleau.

These are still fairly conventionally composed, statically lit works tailored for the Salon. Indeed, at the 1865 Salon, while the scandal raged over Manet's *Olympia*, in the same room Monet's two paintings *The Cape of Le Hève at Low Tide* (1865, Fort Worth, Kimball

Claude MONET, Caricature of
Mario Ochard, c.1856–58, pencil,
Art Institute of Chicago, Gift of Mr
and Mrs Carter H. Harrison.

Art Museum), and *The Seine Estuary at Honfleur* (1865, Pasadena, Norton Simon Foundation) were enjoying considerable success. These contain the merest hints of Monet's mature interests – for example, the glistening reflections on the beach in *The Cape.*

Up to 1866 all Monet's paintings intended for exhibition were painted in the studio using open-air studies and sketches. The problem for him was reconciling the freshness of his preliminary studies with the standards of finish required of the Salon. And in the winter of 1865–6 this difficulty became a crisis with the painting of *The Luncheon on the Grass.*

Inspired by Manet's treatment of the same subject in 1863, Monet's painting attempted to place life-size figures from the fashionable bourgeoisie in a forest setting which would exploit his new interests in the effects of broken, fragmented sunlight. The genre of the painting is derived from Watteau and the 18th-century *fête galante*, but what was new was the scale. The finished canvas was to be a colossal 15 × 20ft (4.8 × 6.2m), thereby elevating modern Parisian picnickers to a scale worthy of ancient Greek soldiers in an academic history painting.

During the spring and summer of 1865 Monet made several open-air studies in the forest of Fontainebleau and, back in the studio, by September he had completed a large sketch. That October and throughout the winter Monet struggled in Bazille's studio to complete the full-size canvas. But recreating on a monumental scale the sketch's delicate interaction of light and colour seemed to pose insurmountable problems, and Monet was eventually forced to abandon the project. Only two fragments of the unfinished painting survive (both are now housed in the Musée d'Orsay, Paris) after it had been left, literally, to rot.

Undeterred by this setback, Monet continued to experiment with light and colour. His commitment to the ideals of open-air painting reach heroic proportions with his *Women in the Garden* (1866, Paris, Musée d'Orsay), which at 8½ × 6½ft [2.6 × 1.9m] must be one of the largest paintings ever executed entirely out of doors. To achieve this, Monet had to dig a trench in his Paris suburban garden and lower the canvas into the trench to reach the upper sections of the canvas. The same model, his companion and future wife Camille, was used for all the figures in the painting, her elegant dresses reflecting contemporary fashion prints. As Zola pointed out, Monet's vision of the country at this time was of a place for the fashion-

Claude MONET, Luncheon on
the Grass *(fragment), c.1865–66,
Paris, Musée d'Orsay.*

....
Claude MONET, The Bodmer
Oak at the Bas-Breau,
Fontainebleau Forest, *1865, New
York, Metropolitan Museum of Art,
Gift of Sam Salz and bequest of Julia
W. Emmons.*
....

able city dweller's recreation; he was unable to paint it without peopling it with Parisian ladies and gentlemen dressed up *á la mode*.

But the painting is more than a mere fashion parade. Monet's loose, asymmetric placing of the figures is entirely his own, as is his preoccupation with different types and intensities of light and shade (the latter now tinged with green or violet). This second attempt to monumentalize bourgeois life was duly rejected by the 1867 Salon jury.

For Monet, the years 1867-70 combined humiliating poverty with a growing assurance of artistic vision. He and Camille led a peripatetic life, eking out their meagre income with the contributions of friends such as Bazille and Renoir. Yet this could hardly be guessed from the summery mood of *Terrace at Sainte-Adresse* (1867, New York, Metropolitan Museum of Art). This painting already exhibits, in raw form, some of the elements of Monet's mature Impressionism such as a 'Japanese' viewpoint with a strong horizontal emphasis, and vivid highlights of pure colour. For all its seeming bourgeois tranquillity, *Terrace* was painted in 1867, when Monet's financial straits had forced him to return to his parent's house leaving Camille with friends to give birth to their son.

Monet's accelerating originality at this period can be further gauged by comparing *The Magpie* [1868-9, Paris, Musée d'Orsay], an early masterpiece rejected by the Salon of 1869, with *Landscape under Snow* of c.1867 [Paris, Louvre] by Courbet, one of the more progressive landscape painters of the mid 19th century (particularly in his use of the palette knife). Courbet's near-monochrome landscape is dramatized by strong tonal contrasts, the white paint being laid

....
A B O V E
Jean–Antoine WATTEAU, Fête in a
Park, *c.1720, London, Wallace
Collection.*
....

O P P O S I T E
Claude MONET, The Magpie,
1868–8, Paris, Musée d'Orsay.
....

thickly over the dark ground to suggest physically the
effects of snow-covered earth. In Monet's scene the
snow covering is indicated by the use of light and
shadow. The shadow of the wattle fence is painted
with a delicate interplay of pale lilacs, and the snow
itself is not pure white but a mixture of whites enlivened by spots of light yellow and pink. The effect
of this interplay is reinforced by Monet unifying,
rather than contrasting, the tone of sky and snow.

Despite the depth of snow depicted and the scale of
the canvas, it is quite likely that most, if not all of *The
Magpie* was painted in the open air. The extent of
Monet's commitment to open-air painting can be
gauged from an article published in 1868 by a local
Normandy journalist: 'We have only seen him once. It
was in the winter, during several days of snow, when
communications were virtually at a standstill. It was
cold enough to split stones. We noticed a foot-
warmer, then an easel, then a man, swathed in three
coats, his hands in gloves, his face half froze. It was
M. Monet studying a snow effect. Art has its brave
soldiers.'

In the summer of 1869, Monet's progress towards
the type of painting that we now call Impressionism
was all but achieved in his scenes of La Grenouillère,
painted in preparation for yet another ambitious
entry to the Salon. La Grenouillère was a bathing
resort and restaurant six miles (ten kilometres) outside Paris which had become popular with trippers
following the building of the railway in 1850. It

Claude MONET, Terrace at Sainte-Adresse, *1867, New York, Metropolitan Museum of Art.*

became especially crowded on Sundays and was associated with social activities of dubious morality – La Grenouillère meant 'frog pond', but more colloquially, 'tart'.

Monet was joined by Renoir (whose parents lived nearby), and the two of them set up their easels, virtually painting side by side. Two of Monet's sketches of La Grenouillère survive (London, National Gallery and New York, Metropolitan Museum). A third composition, which may have been that submitted to the Salon in 1870, was destroyed in Berlin during World War II.

In a letter to Bazille in September, 1869 Monet modestly dismissed the results of his visits to La Grenouillère as some bad *pochades* – an academic term for a sketch which captures the correct values of a whole scene.

Monet's paintings of La Grenouillère have rightly been regarded as crucial in the formation of Impressionism as a style, but ironically they use a format from the academic curriculum in preparation for a Salon painting.

The theme of *La Grenouillère* united the earliest strands of Monet's career – trees, water, and above all, light. In his sketch in the National Gallery, London, he deliberately avoids almost all direct lighting, concentrating instead on the interplay of light breaking through the trees and reflecting off water. The painting is also radical in its composition: the boats in the foreground are cut off to lead the observer's eye into space, but this is offset by the 'flattening'

....

Claude MONET, La Grenouillère
1869, London, National Gallery.
This popular resort, situated on the
Île de Croissy, facing the left bank of
the Seine, is here seen in the
afternoon, looking north-east. Monet
dismissed the picture as 'a bad
pochade', *but significantly the boat*
on the right has been added later to
balance the composition.

....

effect of the jetty which cuts the picture in half; this device is not unusual in Japanese art, but was exceptional in the West which was used to the 'harmonious' principles of the Golden Section. But it is Monet's approach to colour that makes this painting the real precursor of Impressionism. Pigment is applied direct from the tube, such as the vermilion of the flowers and lady's dress on the left; colours are mixed on the canvas itself (as in the foliage in the centre); the luminosity of the 'green' shadows of the boats under the trees is achieved by mixing green with its complementary colour, red; the flickering surface of the water is 'modelled' with individual blocks of pure colour, rejecting orthodox tonal modelling. The whole, broadly treated, scene is alive with the bustle of a modern crowd at play.

Monet's admissions to the 1870 Salon were *The Luncheon* (1868, Frankfurt, Staedelisches Kunstinstitut) and a landscape, which may have been the destroyed Berlin *La Grenouillère*. Both were once again rejected.

It was this 1870 rejection which finally resolved Monet to abandon his time-consuming submissions to the Salon, and he did not present them a painting again for a decade. He dispensed with the 'finished' studio *tableau*, concentrating instead on small-scale paintings, executed entirely in the open air, which would retain the spontaneity of a sketch. It was this decision that heralded the birth of Impressionism.

CHAPTER THREE

THE NEW GENERATION

Paul CÉZANNE, Portrait of
Achille Emperaire, *c.1868–70,
Paris, Musée d'Orsay.*

Courbet was still the tradition, but Manet was the new generation of painting.' Renoir's well-known, if apocryphal, tribute points not only to Manet's individual artistic achievement, but also his role as the standard-bearer for the Parisian avant-garde. From October 1864 Manet lived at 34 Boulevard des ·Batignolles, one of the main thoroughfares of the Batignolles district of Paris which extended roughly from Gare St Lazare to the Montmartre Cemetery, an area well known for its relatively cheap rents. From 1866 onwards Manet began to frequent the Café Guerbois at 11 Grade Rue des Batignolles (later to be known as Avenue Clichy), and this soon became the rallying point for those involved with the new, independently minded painting. Artists such as Fantin-Latour, Degas, Pissarro, Cézanne, the photographer Nadar, the critics Zola, Silvestre, Duranty, and Duret – all were regular visitors to the café, where Manet would hold court on the Thursday evenings set aside for the regular meetings of his *bande*. These gatherings were reinforced early in 1868 by the arrival of Monet, who in turn brought Renoir, Bazille, and Sisley, his friends from student days at the *atelier* Gleyre. By the spring of 1868 Zola was able to refer in his journalism to a fairly clearly defined 'Batignolles Group'.

Although virtually nothing was recorded of what was discussesd at the Café Guerbois, it must have been there, around its marble-topped tables, that many of the principles of Impressionism were forged. The social mixture itself was combustible enough. The haughty, witty Degas, proclaiming 'the unsuitability of making art available to the working classes', was thrown together with the anarchist Pissarro, and the pleasure-loving Renoir who was sceptical of all theoretical discussion. And there was Manet himself, urbane, fastidious, having to confront Cézanne, the *enfant terrible* of the Paris Salon who reputedly once said 'I won't offer you my hand, Monsieur Manet, I haven't washed for eight days.' (John Rewald, *The History of Impressionism*, Secker & Warburg, 1973.)

L E F T Henri FANTIN-LATOUR,
A Studio in the Batignolles
Quarter, *1870, Paris, Musée*
d'Orsay. Manet works in his studio
surrounded by a band of admirers.

....

A B O V E Frédéric BAZILLE, A
Studio in the Rue Condamine,
1870, Paris, Musée d'Orsay. Manet
scrutinizes a painting watched by
Monet and the immensely tall Bazille.

....

It was to be Monet and the friends he had made at Gleyre's studio who were to form the inner core of the Impressionist group. After their exodus from the studio in 1863, Monet, Renoir, Bazille and Sisley kept in contact with each other throughout the 1860s, often painting together and sharing studios. In 1867 an amiable Bazille wrote to his parents: 'Monet has fallen upon me from the skies with a collection of magnificent canvases ... Counting Renoir, that makes two hard-working painters I'm housing.'

Shortly afterwards Bazille moved with Renoir to a large studio in the Rue de la Paix (later re-named Rue de la Condamine) where Sisley was living in the same building. This *ménage* was commemorated by Bazille in his *Studio in the rue de la Condamine* (1870, Paris, Musee d'Orsay). Sharing and visiting each other's Paris studios was combined with regular *plein air* sketching expeditions to the suburbs of Paris and beyond. A favourite haunt was the forest of Fontaine-bleau, and in particular the village of Marlotte, where the Inn of Mother Anthony specialized in the accommodation of painters working *en plein air*.

These processes of cross-fertilization between Monet, Renoir, Sisley and Bazille produced eclectic results during the 1860s. Before Monet's creation of a developed Impressionist idioim at La Grenouillère in 1869, their paintings struggled to break away from the presiding influences of Courbet, Corot and the Barbizon School. For example, although little of Sisley's early work survives, his *Montmartre from the Cité des Fleurs* (1869, Grenoble, Musée des Beaux-

Arts) dated relatively late, still shows the muted colour range and formal device of silhouetted trees used by Corot; sky and land are as yet not unified atmospherically; colour is unbroken. However, Sisley's choice of an almost uninhabited, wide open space – in this case one of surburban desolation – is one of the trademarks of his maturer works of the 1870s.

Sisley possessed, like his paintings, an elusive, solitary character and was an infrequent visitor to the Café Guerbois. This contrasted with the easy-going affability of Renoir who, like Sisley, had enrolled at the official Ecole des Beaux-Arts as well as Gleyre's studio. Renoir's earliest training at the age of 15 had been as a porcelain painter with the Paris firm of Levy Brothers, an influence not to be underestimated in assessing his feathery brushwork, his use of thin 'glazes' of colour floated into each other wet-in-wet, and his sheer sensitivity to decorative pattern.

Renoir's paintings of the 1860s are an uneasy mixture of compositions which attempted to ingratiate themselves with the Salon jury, and freer, more personal works which express a forward-looking treatment of light and atmosphere. Renoir's two idioms met with a paradoxical response from the Salon jury. His *Diana the Huntress* (1867, Washington DC, National Gallery) – modelled by Renoir's companion Lise Tréhot – is a subject treated by Gleyre in his mythological confections, while the heavy, 'bourgeois' proportions of the nude, the deer at her feet, and the conspicuous use of the palette knife are all reminiscent of Courbet. Despite seeming to be tailor-made for the Salon, the *Diana* was rejected by the 1867 jury, presumably because of its sensuous rendition of flesh and powerful frontal lighting.

More radical in approach was Renoir's *Lise* (1867, Essen, Folkwang Museum) which was accepted by the Salon jury of 1868, thanks to the benign intervention of Daubigny (who had been absent the previous year). In this painting, a modern lady of fashion is convincingly integrated into an outdoor setting. She stands half in light, half in shade which is tinged with the greenness of the trees that surround her. The critic Burger commented perceptively in that year's Salon review: 'The effect is so natural, so true that no one might very well find it false . . . Does not colour depend upon the environment that surrounds it?' (Rewald, *The History of Impressionism.*)

Although Renoir had a comparatively high success rate with the Salon jury, in common with other progressively minded artists of the 1860s, he realized the

....
Alfred SISLEY, Montartre from
the Cité des Fleurs, *1869,*
Grenoble, Musée des Beaux-Arts.
....

iniquity of the Salon being the only major venue where an as-yet-unestablished painter could exhibit his work. With the notable exception of Daubigny, the Salon jury itself maintained an exclusionist stance towards dangerously 'progressive' painting. The jury of 1867 (without Daubigny) had been exceptionally severe, rejecting not only Renoir's *Diana,* but also Monet's *Women in the Garden.*

Bazille's entries for the 1867 Salon were also rejected, and in May of that year he wrote to his parents describing what must have been one of the major subjects of discussion at the Café Guerbois, the mounting of an independent exhibition.

The following year Daubigny returned to the Salon jury and, thanks to his influence, Bazille's rather stiff *Family Reunion* (1867, Paris, Musee d'Orsay) was accepted, together with works by Manet,

Degas, Monet, Sisley, Renoir and Berthe Morisot. But a year later, after having one painting accepted by the jury and one refused, the revolutionary idea of an independent group exhibition was aired again in a letter to his parents. Tragically, Bazille's plans – and life – were to be curtailed by political events.

On 14 July, 1870, using Bismarck's supposed designs on the Spanish throne as a *casus belli,* France mobilized its army against Prussia. This venture was in reality an ill-advised attempt by Napoleon III to divert attention from the domestic problems that had followed an economic recession in 1857–8; but instead it was to provide the humiliating climax to a decade's blundering foreign policy. The French hurriedly assembled an army of 200,000 troops, led personally by the Emperor himself, to confront a Prussian enemy which could draw on huge trained reserves, and

Frédéric BAZILLE, Family
Reunion, *1867, Paris, Musée
d'Orsay.*

which four years previously had been battle-hardened in crushing Austria.

The campaign was an unmitigated disaster for France. Within six weeks the Emperor and an army of 84,000 troops had surrendered at Sedan. Bismarck next marched on Paris, laying siege to the city for four months in an attempt to starve its inhabitants into submission. On 28 January, 1871 – with Paris still holding out, its inhabitants forced to live on horse and rat meat – the French government signed a humiliating armistice. The following March, Parisian radicals exploited the groundswell of popular feeling against the former regime by establishing a new socialist government in Paris – the Commune. A mere two months later, under the watchful eyes of the Prussians, French government troops led by Napoleon III's former minister of the Interior, Adolphe Thiers, stormed Paris. The Commune was suppressed mercilessly; 100,000 Parisians were killed, imprisoned, or exiled; many of those killed were des-patched in mass shootings; women and children were bayonetted; and an elderly bourgeois, one Léon Colin, wrote to Thiers calling for mass exterminations and volunteered for the honour of participating in firing squads. 'So far as we can recollect,' wrote *The Times* 'there has been nothing like it in history.'

The Franco-Prussian war inevitably dispersed the nascent Impressionist group identity. Too old for active service, Manet and Degas stayed in Paris where they joined the artillery of the National Guard. Sisley remained with his family in Louveciennes – a suburban village 10 miles (16km) west of Paris, where Monet, Renoir and Pissarro had worked before the war – faced with the prospect of having to paint for a living after the bankruptcy and death of his father in 1870. Cézanne escaped southwards to L'Estaque, a coastal village near Marseilles. Renoir was declared fit for active service, but was drafted too late to see action. Bazille was less lucky. He had enlisted with the Zouaves, a unit legendary for its fearlessness under fire. On 20 November, 1870, while retreating at Beaune-la-Rolande, Bazille was shot dead by a Prussian sniper. Meanwhile, Monet escaped to England – as did Pissarro.

....
Camille PISSARRO, The
Towpath, *Glasgow Art Gallery and
Museum, 1864. A rare survival of both
an open-air study (etude) and the studio-
executed finished painting (tableau).*
....

Born in the West Indies of a Creole mother and a French father of Portuguese-Jewish descent, Camille Pissarro (1831–1903) had first arrived in France at the age of 24 in 1855. After enrolling in the Ecole des Beaux Arts he had come under the influence of Corot. Over the next decade, independently of the other Impressionists, he had slowly evolved his own naturalistic response to landscape. By 1868 his Salon submissions were being praised by Zola, with typical hyperbole, for their 'epic grandeur' and he had become a fairly regular, if diffident, visitor to the Café Guerbois. The turning point in Pissarro's artistic career had come in 1869 – that *annus mirabilis* in the history of Impressionism – when he had moved to Louveciennes, where Monet and Renoir were both living. Here, painting in the open air with these two leading exponents of the Parisian avant garde, Pissarro's work assumed a new compositional inform-ality and lightness of touch. Unfortunately, charting this transformation is hindered by the fact that

during the Franco-Prussian war, the Prussian army who used his house as a butcher's shop during the occupation destroyed an estimated 1,500 paintings. Several slightly later works from Pissarro's Louveciennes period do survive, by which time his new, proto-Impressionistic manner had been substantially developed.

Monet and Pissarro lived in London each unaware of the other's presence until they were put in contact through the offices of Paul Durand-Ruel, a French picture dealer and fellow refugee, who had opened a gallery in New Bond Street. Durand-Ruel had been a tireless supporter of the Barbizon painters (among whom Daubigny was also in London) and was to become the earliest, and most important, commercial agent of the Impressionists.

Once contact had been made, Monet and Pissarro met frequently. Together they visited London's museums where they admired, with reservations, the works of Constable and Turner (their treatment of shadows and Turner's Romantic excess came in for particular criticism). Monet and Pissarro also had the idea of sending their studies to the exhibition at the Royal Academy. These were rejected, but the painters were represented, thanks to the intervention of Durand-Ruel, in the French section of the 1871 International Exhibition at South Kensington.

The works of the two artists at this period – significantly still referred to by Pissarro as *études* – make an interesting contrast. Monet's studies of London parks (an unusual subject in itself at that date) capture the quality of the city's light with an atmospheric exactitude beyond the powers of any contemporary English artist. The colour of 19th-century London is subdued; each study is a broadly handled essay in tonal modulation enlivened by acutely observed human detail. While Monet concentrated on painting central London, Pissarro, who had settled in Lower Norwood, painted its suburbs. Where the colours of Monet's palette were subdued in order to record the 'English-

ness of English light', Pissarro's become more vivid (almost unaccountably, given the monochromatic drabness of most London suburbs). In Pissarro's *The Avenue, Sydenham*, (1871, London, National Gallery) the artist adopts his favourite view from the side of a road which recedes into the distance. But his previous compositional formula of intersecting diagonals beneath a stabilizing horizon has now been broken up by trees and figures; these figures themselves are now no longer static compositional props, but are full of movement and human interest. Pissarro's works of the 1860s had maintained an awkward balance between a scene naturalistically observed and his expressive use of thickly applied, almost glutinous oil paint; in *The Avenue at Sydenham* the paint is thinner, more evenly applied, the touch more spontaneous. But above all, it is in the painting's use of colour that we can appreciate what Pissarro has gained from his association with Monet and Renoir. The colour has a higher 'key' than his previous works, even those executed at Louveciennes; the almost lurid green of the right-hand verge is applied thin and flat, without tonal 'modelling'; and, just as Monet had done in the later 1860s, vivid accents of red and blue are used to animate the overall effect.

Pissarro returned to France in June 1871, having married Julie Vellay, the former maid of his parents' household . She had already borne him a son, and they would eventually have six more children. In the summer of the following year Pissarro settled a few miles north-east of Paris in the village of Pontoise where he was joined by Cézanne. As with Gauguin later, Pissarro's crucial influence brought about a fundamental change in Cézanne's artistic outlook.

Cézanne had been an old school-friend of Zola in Aix-en-Provence, and like Zola was determined to make a name for himself in the Parisian art world. Many of Cézanne's works in the 1860s were nightmare visions which owed much compositionally to his idol Delacroix; they were ferociously painted with a palette knife in what he termed his *couillarde* manner. These inevitably made Cézanne the *bête noire* of the artistic establishment; he stubbornly accumulated a total of 15 Salon rejections from 1863–86, and was accepted only once, in 1882.

The Black Clock of 1869–70 (London, Stavros Niarchos Collection) is one of Cézanne's early masterpieces which already shows a feeling – in its emphatic foreground verticals – for solid, structured composition. It is charged with sinister overtones, the uncom-

fortably lurid blood red of the conch shell juxtaposed with the blackness of the clock, and the clock itself has no hands.

The Black Clock was a highly original composition, but its tonal values were fundamentally still those of a Salon painting. However, from around 1872, under instruction from Pissarro, Cézanne's palette and touch lighten. Pissarro advised Cézanne to abandon blacks, bitumens and earth colours, to paint instead with the three primary colours and their immediate derivatives.

Pissarro seems to have been responsible for a transformation in Cézanne's psychological outlook as well. The dark, claustrophobic and violent inner world that had so dominated Cézanne's output in the 1860s is left behind in a re-discovery of the external, natural world. *The House of the Hanged Man* (1872–3, Paris, Musée d'Orsay) is one of Cézanne's first mature landscapes. The overall tonality is lighter, as is the texture of paint which is applied in subtly alternating areas of brush and palette knife. The menace still remains in the choice of motif (the house of a man who committed suicide), but the emotional power has now been harnessed to create a composition of taut geometry and monumentally solid forms.

Monet, in contrast, had developed in a different direction. In the summer of 1871 he had left England for Holland where he perhaps hoped to meet Daubigny. It was in Holland, which had traditional trading links with Japan through the port of Nagasaki, that Monet was first able to purchase Japanese prints – thanks to the proceeds of paintings sold to Durand-Ruel in London. The effect of Japanese prints on Monet's work was immediate. Several of his works from the 1860s had shown generalized compositional

debts to the art of Japan, but in Holland Monet began to exploit the bright, 'flat' colours of Japanese prints. The greyest canalscape is vivified with broad slabs of pure, high-keyed colour.

In November 1871, Monet returned to a Paris still bearing the scars of war: the humiliating peace treaty that the government had signed the previous May obliged France to pay a five billion franc indemnity, surrender the rich provinces of Alsace and Lorraine, and allow German troops a triumphal march through the streets of Paris. In the face of this national debasement, patriotic and economic regeneration was surprisingly rapid. The five billion franc indemnity was paid off by public subscription in only two-and-a-half years. Paris monuments destroyed during the Commune – which included the Hôtel de Ville, Palais des Tuileries, Bibliothèque du Louvre, and the Vendôme Column – were restored or reconstructed; and in the fervour of regeneration new monuments were commissioned, the most famous being the Sacré Coeur, Montmartre.

In the general headiness of patriotic optimism, Monet, Pissarro *et al* once again aired the idea of an independent exhibition, and this time succeeded in setting it up, in 1874.

One of the misconceptions concerning the first Impressionist exhibition of 1874 is that it took place in an atmosphere of establishment hostility against progressive art. In fact, in the aftermath of the Franco-Prussian war, and with the stirrings of re-generation, there was a general realization among officialdom, critics, and even the audience, of the Salon's limitations and the need for independently organized group exhibitions. Indeed, Charles Blanc, before being forced by conservative elements to re-sign his appointment as 'Directeur des Beaux-Arts' in 1873, had advocated two Salons, one organized by the state, the other by the artists. In effect this institution-alized the Salon des Refusés.

Although the idea for what was to become known as the first Impressionist exhibition can be traced back to Bazille's letters in 1867, it was only in the

Claude MONET, Zaandam, 1871, Private Collection. Monet's rediscovery of Japanese prints in Holland inspired a more vividly coloured palette.

Edouard MANET, Bon Bock (Good Beer), 1873, Philadelphia Museum of Art, Mr and Mrs Carroll S. Tyson Collection. The picture was bought by the singer and composer Fauré for 6000 francs.

summer of 1873 that it started to become a reality. The group was formally constituted – using a charter based on the one adopted by the baker's union of Pissarro's home town Pontoise – on 27 December, 1873, as the *Société anonyme coopérative d'artistes-peintres sculpteurs graveurs etc.* There appear to have been 16 founding members, who included Monet, Sisley, Degas, Renoir, Pissarro and Morisot, supplemented (at the suggestion of Degas) by painters such as the Vicomte Ludovic-Napoléon Lepic, Auguste de Molins and Jean-Baptiste Léopold Levert. These latter, now obscure, Salon painters had been included in an attempt to give the new breakaway group establishment credibility.

Claude MONET, Boulevard des Capucines, 1873, Moscow, Puskin Museum. This is one of two versions, the other being in Kansas City, The Nelson-Atkins Museum.

Manet did not exhibit at this first Impressionist exhibition, declaring that 'The Salon is the real field of battle. It's there one must take one's measure.' (Rewald, *The History of Impressionism.*) The previous year he had shown himself to be a reluctant iconoclast by exhibiting *Bon Bock* (1873, Philadelphia Museum of Art) at the Salon. This retrogressive portrait of the engraver Bellot, based on memories of Frans Hals' paintings seen by Manet when he visited Holland in 1872, tasted considerable critical success at the Salon – a triumph Manet commemorated by painting a beer mug on the palette he had used.

The first exhibition of the *Société Anonyme* opened on 15 April, two weeks before the official Salon, in the recently vacated studios of the photographer Nadar at 35 Boulevard des Capucines. Entrance to the exhibition cost one franc, the catalogue 50 centimes, and to maximize the potential attendance the show stayed open until 10pm during its month duration. But despite its well-known venue and careful planning, the exhibition attracted only 3,500 visitors, many of whom came only to laugh.

More than 200 works by 39 artists were hung (and placed, since the exhibition also included several pieces of sculpture) by Renoir against a background of red-brown flocked wallpaper. Most of the attention, serious and otherwise, was inevitably focussed on the 50 or so entries by the core of seven Impressionists – Monet, Pissarro, Sisley, Morisot, Degas, Renoir and Cézanne. The prices of their paintings were surprisingly high. Encouraged by successful prices achieved by Monet and Pissarro in the Drouot auction rooms, and by the investments of Durand-Ruel (who by the end of 1873 had spent 70,000 francs on Impressionist paintings), Monet had the temerity to place a price tag of 1,000 francs on his notorious *Impression: Sunrise*. The same price was placed on

Pierre-Auguste RENOIR, La Loge
(The Theatre Box), *1874,*
London, Courtauld Institutute
Galleries.

Alfred *SISLEY*, Autumn: Banks of
the Seine near Bougival, *1873,*
Bequest of Miss Adaline Van Horne,
Montreal Museum of Fine Arts.

Pissarro's *Le Verger* (1872, Washington, National Gallery of Art).

The critical response was mixed. Emile Cardon may have dismissively announced that 'the debaucheries' of the group were 'nauseating and revolting', but the majority of the critics approved of the idea of an independent exhibition; their responses to individual works, however, was often less positive. The most prolonged invective came from Louis Leroy in the humorous journal *Le Charivari,* in which he declared himself mystified by the 'black tongue lickings' of Monet's *Boulevard des Capucines* (1873, Kansas City, Nelson Atkins Museum) and in which he coined the very term Impressionism, used in a derogatory way, when confronted with Monet's *Impression: Sunrise.* In contrast, Ernest Chesneau, who had catalogued the Impressionist works at the successful sale at the Hôtel Drouot in January of that year, and who wrote no fewer than six articles about the first exhibition, hailed Monet's *Boulevard des Capucines* as a masterpiece. Chesneau went on to praise the remarkable colour qualities of Renoir's *La Loge* (1874, London, Courtauld Institute Galleries). Berthe Morisot's *Hide and Seek* (1873, New York, Collection Mrs John Hay Whitney) was applauded by *La République* for its observation, freshness of colour, and composition. But more representative of the critics' generally lukewarm response to the Impressionists was Pierre Toloza's review of Sisley's contributions to the exhibition. *Autumn: Banks of the Seine near Bougival* (1873, Montreal, Museum of Fine Arts) was singled out as 'a charming work', but his other paintings were dismissed as 'mediocre canvases'.

In the aftermath of the Franco-Prussian war, the critics and public alike recognized that art had an important part to play in the nation's regeneration. Recognizing the paintings that were actually regenerating French art was proving rather more difficult.

CHAPTER FOUR

HIGH SUMMER

Pierre-Auguste RENOIR, The
Gust of Wind, *c.1873, Cambridge,
Fitzwilliam Museum.*

During the period 1874–86 the Impressionists held a total of eight independent exhibitions. This number might have been expected to improve the critical and public reception to their works, to increase prices on the open market, and to establish Impressionism as a force which the academic establishment would have to recognize. In fact it appeared to have quite the opposite effect. During the later 1870s, painters without private incomes, such as Pissarro, Sisley, Renoir and Monet, had to endure protracted bouts of crippling poverty – at times Monet's begging letters were almost as dogged and prolific as his painting.

The numbing effects of seemingly perpetual obscurity forced all of them – bar the heroic Pissarro, who was the only artist of the group to participate in all eight Impressionist exhibitions – into submitting their works to the Salon jury, thus forfeiting their right to be included in the independent exhibition (if one was held that year). In the 1870s Renoir regularly submitted to the Salon in those years without an Impressionist exhibition, achieving success in the 1879 Salon with his portrait of *Madame Charpentier and her Children* (1878, New York, Metropolitan Museum of Art); that same year a desperate Sisley entered two works into the Salon, both of which were refused. In 1880 Monet, virtually penniless, and at the end of his tether after the death of his wife, submitted two large river views. Only one was accepted, and then badly hung.

During this same period, even those artists of independent means, such as Manet, Degas, Cézanne and Morisot, were finding it increasingly difficult to market their paintings. Following a financial crash in

1873 and an ensuing six-year recession, the dealer Durand-Ruel was forced to curtail his buying of Impressionist works. The small number of private buyers was also dwindling: Ernest Hoschedé, the director of a Paris department store, patron of Monet and substantial collector of the new paintings, was financially ruined by 1878; and Victor Chocquet, who had developed a life-long enthusiasm for the Impressionists, was by the later 1870s reduced to giving moral rather than financial support.

The market value of Impressionist works actually fell during the 1870s. The surprisingly high prices achieved at auction in 1874 by paintings from Hoschedé's collection (a Sisley fetched 575 francs, a Degas an even more surprising 1,100) proved to be a false dawn. The following year, in an attempt to capture new private clients, the Impressionists under the aegis of Durand-Ruel took the unusual step of mounting their own sale at the Hôtel Drouot. The event was later described by Durand-Ruel:

In the course of the sale there was a fine commotion, I must say. The insults which were hurled at us – especially Monet and Renoir! The public howled, and treated us as imbeciles, as people with no sense of decency. Works were sold for as little as 50 francs – and that was only because of the frames. (*Impressionists at First Hand*, Ed Bernard, Denvir, London, 1987.)

....
OPPOSITE Pierre-Auguste RENOIR, Portrait of Madame Charpentier and her Children, *1878, New York, Metropolitan Museum of Art.*
....
ABOVE | *Camille PISSARRO*, Red Roofs, *1877, Paris, Musée d'Orsay.*
....

A second Hoschedé sale in June 1878, held as a result of his insolvency, produced even more disastrous results. Pissarro's works fared worst. In the 1874 sale Pissarro had been heartened when two of his canvases reached 700 and 950 francs respectively; in 1878 his entry of nine canvases fetched a total of only 404 francs, including one sold for a mere seven francs, and another for 10. That year, in common with Monet and Sisley, Pissarro was being hounded by creditors, only his situation was compounded by the fact that his wife was expecting a fourth child. In a letter to Eugène Murer, a restauranteur who was one of the Impressionists' few remaining private buyers, he described his desperate situation and even wondered if he could try his hand at doing something else. Yet how little this mood seems to accord with Pissarro's works of the period, such as his vibrant *Red Roofs* which had been painted in 1877 and exhibited in the third Impressionist exhibition of that year. It is only when one contemplates the feverish re-working

of the paint on the right-hand side of the composition – praised now, a little anachronistically, for its 'abstract' qualities – that one can sense Pissarro's anxiety.

Pissarro's *Red Roofs* is representative of the so-called 'High' Impressionism of the mid-to-late 1870s. It was during this period that the Impressionists, sometimes in the face of great personal deprivation, gave the purest, most quintessential expression to their artistic principles. But what were these principles?

Despite the general public's hostility, by the mid 1870s a group of critics had grown which was sympathetic to the tenets of Impressionism. To long-standing stalwarts such as Zola and Théodore Duret could be added the playwright and librettist Armand Silvestre, who had written an introduction to Durand-Ruel's 1873 catalogue distinguishing between the respective qualities of Monet, Pissarro and Sisley. In 1876 the poet Stéphane Mallarmé published his laudatory *The Impressionists and Edouard Manet* in a London periodical, and in the same year the critic

....

A B O V E

Edgar DEGAS, Portrait of
Edmond Duranty, *The Burrell
Collection, Glasgow Art Gallery and
Museum. Louis Emile Edmond
Duranty (1833–80) was a literary
figure best known for his essay 'The
New Painting: Concerning the
Group of Artists Exhibiting at the
Durand-Ruel Galleries'.*

....

O P P O S I T E Alfred SISLEY, The
Weir at Molesey, *1874, Edinburgh,
National Galleries of Scotland.*

....

Edmond Duranty published a pamphlet entitled *The New Painting: Concerning the Group of Artists Exhibiting at the Durand-Ruel Galleries.* This praised the modernity of his friend Degas (without naming the artist), but expressed misgivings about the Impressionists (without using the term).

However, the most incisive, definitive analysis of Impressionist painting was to come from the pen of Jules Laforgue (1860–87), a brilliant, but tragically short-lived Symbolist poet. Laforgue wrote a brief introduction for a small exhibition at the Gurlitt Gallery in Berlin in October 1883, which included works by Pissarro, Degas, and Renoir. Written in a heady scientific-poetic style, Laforgue's article resembles at times a prophetic manifesto for modernism and is worth quoting at some length:

The Impressionist is . . . a modernist painter endowed with an uncommon sensibility of the eye. He is one who . . . has succeeded in remaking for himself a natural eye, and in seeing naturally and painting simply as he sees . . .

One can point to three supreme illusions by which technicians of painting have always lived: *line, perspective, studio lighting.* To these three things, which have become second nature to the painter, correspond the three steps of the Impressionist formula: form obtained not by line but solely by vibration and contrast of colour; theoretic perspective replaced by the natural perspective of colour vibration and contrast; studio lighting . . . replaced by *plein-air*, open air – that is, by painting done in front of its subject, however impractical, and in the shortest possible time, considering how quickly the light changes . . .

A natural eye forgets tactile illusions and their convenient dead language of line, and acts only in its faculty of prismatic sensibility . . . In a landscape flooded with light . . . where the academic painter sees nothing but a broad expanse of whiteness, the Impressionist sees light as bathing not with a dead whiteness but rather with a thousand vibrant struggling colours of rich prismatic composition . . . where one sees things placed in their regular respective planes . . . the other sees perspective established by a thousand trivial touches of tone and brush, by the varieties of atmospheric states induced by moving planes.

The Impressionist eye is, in short, the most advanced eye in human evolution . . . sees and renders nature as it is – that is, wholly in the vibration of colour. (L. Nochlin, *Impressionism and Post Impressionism: 1874–1904*, Sources & Documents Series, Prentice Hall, 1966.)

In this article, Laforgue referred to the Impressionists' 'prismatic sensibility', a notion which echoed the Turneresque credo of 'painting what I see, not what I know'. This had a scientific basis in the Young-

Herholtz theory of colour vision which isolated three retinal and post-retinal processes; these processes produce sensations of red, yellow, green and blue and all other colours, including white, are blendings of these. Using this theory Laforgue showed academic painters' reproductions of studio-controlled white light to be as artificial as their perspective constructions. He further identified centuries of insidious inter-reaction between these academic devices and the ways in which people looked at the world around them. In other words, the 19th-century spectator was imposing 'academic composition' on his or her perceptions of day-to-day reality. But according to Laforgue, the Impressionist's 'natural eye' pulled away this veil of expectation, evoking the first raw sensations of vision before intellectual ordering.

Laforgue's 'manifesto' rightly pin-pointed the *plein air* landscape painting, executed perhaps only 15

....
Edgar DEGAS, The Dance
Lesson, *c.1879, Upperville,
Virginia, Collection of Mr and Mrs
Paul Mellon. This remarkable
painting was included in the fifth
Impressionist exhibition of 1880 and
described by the critic and novelist
Joris Karl Huysmans as 'dismal'.*
....

minutes at a time, as the quintessential Impressionist medium. This was to be later confirmed by Monet who asserted that no painter could work for more than half an hour on an open-air composition and remain true to nature. From the 1890s Monet would work on a number of canvases simultaneously, returning to a different canvas with each change of atmospheric effect.

Laforgue's essay brilliantly summarized Impressionism as being a highly sophisticated form of naturalism which analyzes in paint one individual's fleeting sensory response to the external world. Looking at some of the 'pure' Impressionist paintings of the 1870s two central elements can be distinguished in this particular way of seeing.

For example, Renoir's *Gust of Wind* (c.1873, Cambridge, Fitzwilliam Museum) can be viewed at one level as a scintillating description of a landscape acti-

vated by strong wind. This would place the composition firmly in the naturalistic tradition of a painting such as Daubigny's *Spring Landscape* (1862, New York, Private Collection). But what distinguishes Renoir's *Gust of Wind* specifically as an Impressionist work is not only its freer handling – using the porcelain painting technique of floating 'glazes' of oil paint across each other wet-in-wet – but its psychological stance. What Renoir is painting is not only a landscape in a gust of wind, but also his own immediate,

raw sensations of that landscape; both he and nature are in flux. His painting is as much the notation of internal responses, as external description. And typically for an Impressionist painting of the earlier 1870s, both responses are mutually inclusive, held in dynamic equipoise.

In choosing to paint in this way, 'to abandon themselves to their personal sensations' as the critic Théodore Duret put it, the Impressionists encountered a central paradox. Obviously there was a considerable time-lapse between the painter's momentary sensory response (ie the mental *impression*) and its relatively laborious physical transcription to canvas. For example, Renoir's *Skiff* (c.1879, London, National Gallery), if it existed at all, must have been to a great extent painted from memory, given that the vessel was sailing past him too fast for him to paint it on the spot. A painting, however quickly executed, remains an illusion of spontaneity. The Impressionists in the 1870s masked this anomaly by using a number of formal and technical devices which enhanced the seeming immediacy of their compositions. For example, in Sisley's *The Weir at Molesey* (c. 1874, Edinburgh, National Gallery of Scotland), traditional systems of perspective are rejected for a dynamic arrangement of vanishing axes – the receding line of

submerged triangular posts, the wooden weir, the diagonal line of the racing water, the shadows of the stepped foreground along which the eye surges into and out of pictorial space. This liveliness is further animated by Sisley's varied brushwork which ranges from the long, impasted strokes of the racing water to the broken, multi-directional treatment of the shifting sky. So composition and brushwork both contribute to the immediacy of a scene which can be taken in by the observer at a single glance.

In figure painting the illusion of immediacy is created with even bolder compositional virtuosity by Degas. By the 1870s Degas had settled on a range of personal 'genres' – ballet scenes, concerts, the toilette, laundresses, the racecourse – which he explored with seemingly limitless powers of invention. He was the first to admit the discrepancy between the artist's mental impression and physical execution, acknowledging that his work was the result of reflection and the study of the Great Masters rather than inspiration, spontaneity or temperament. At times even the physical catalysts for the artist's impression were not

73 — Argenteuil (S.-et-O.) - Bords de la Seine

B. F., PARIS

always necessary to Degas. In a letter to his banker patron Albert Hecht, as late as c.1880, he asked for a pass to a ballet examination, confessing shamefacedly that he had done so many versions of the subject without actually ever having seen it.

This would be difficult for the spectator to guess from Degas' *Dance Lesson* (c.1879, Upperville, Virginia, Paul Mellon Collection), shown in the fifth Impressionist exhibition of 1880. At first glance the composition appears to be full of movement, but closer scrutiny reveals that all the figures are either standing still or sitting down. The moment chosen by Degas is in fact between lessons, with the *rats* – the unglamorous 'hoofers' of the Paris ballet – hanging around, killing time. The animation of the scene is generated by its 'open' asymmetrical composition which combines a telescoped multiple-viewpoint, bold truncations of figures, intense colour accents, and daringly large expanses of bare wall and floor. Such devices can be found in 19th-century Japanese woodblock prints, although in this particular case the wide multiple-viewpoint and shape of the painting are also reminiscent of earlier Chinese and Japanese paintings (such as were found on screens).

An admirer of Ingres, Degas' illusions of the captured moment are achieved in *The Dance Lesson* pre-dominantly by its composition, line and tone. But Degas was also an admirer of Delacroix, and his debt to the great Romantic's virtuoso colourism was detected by critics in his *Portrait of Edmond Duranty* (1879, Glasgow, Burrell Collection), also included in the 1880 exhibition. Again, what is essentially a static, monumental arrangement of the sitter among books, is galvanized by an audacious viewpoint. This expressiveness of composition is heightened by Degas using the manufactured blues, reds, oranges and greens of Duranty's book-covers to create 'flat' expanses of colour which tint the painting's reflected light – touches of ultramarine pastel crayon are conspicuous in the shadows beneath the sitter's left hand.

It is perhaps significant that in both Degas' *Dance Lesson* and his *Portrait of Edmond Duranty* the colours used to animate the composition derive from synthetic materials such as the ballet dancer's dyed silks or the publisher's tinted paper covers. Degas' concentration on the man-made environment was once admitted to his Impressionist colleagues when he

Although rarely suggested by Monet's output, Argenteuil in the early 1870s was an industrialized satellite of some 8000 people.

compared their need for natural life with his for artificial life.

Natural life was, of course, Monet's domain. From 1871–78 Monet lived in Argenteuil, a semi-industrial, semi-suburban riverside satellite-town five miles (8 km) outside Paris. Here he produced more than 150 canvases, many from the studio boat that he used from 1873 onwards, probably in emulation of Daubigny's famous *botin,* and was visited periodically by Renoir, Sisley and Manet. Monet's influence resulted in Manet producing the first purely Impressionist works of his career, such as *The River at Argenteuil* (1874, London, National Gallery) and perhaps culminating four years later in his *Roadmenders in the Rue de Berne* (1878, formerly collection of Lord Butler of Saffron Waldon [on loan to Courtauld Collection]; sold Sotheby's, 1987).

By painting from his floating studio Monet was able to dispense with traditional compositional devices such as *repoussoirs* (foreground 'lead-ins') and concentrate instead on the transient effects of colour and light on the river itself. The paintings resulting from this period are of an almost bewildering variety in their appearance.

At one extreme lies *Vétheuil in the Fog* (1879, Paris, Musée Marmottan), a painting with such a limited colour range that it was rejected by one of Monet's patrons, the singer Fauré, because it was almost wholly white, and did not have enough paint on it. (By the 1870s Monet himself considered such an open air *impression* 'complete' enough for sale.) This painting later acquired an almost talismatic quality for Monet; he refused all offers to sell it, keeping it on an easel in his first studio to symbolize the misunderstanding his earlier works had received.

As a rapidly executed essay in tonal modulation, Monet's *Vétheuil in the Fog* can be seen as a highly refined successor to his *Westminster Bridge* (1871,

....
OPPOSITE
Edouard MANET, Claude
Monet and his wife on his
Floating Studio, *1874,*
Munich, Neue Pinakothek.
....
ABOVE
Edouard MANET, The
River at Argenteuil, *1874,*
London, National Gallery.
....
LEFT
Edouard MANET,
Roadmenders in the Rue
de Berne, *1878, formerly*
Collection of Lord Butler of
Saffron Waldon, sold
Sotheby's, 1987.
....

London, National Gallery), with the mist reducing forms and *chiaroscuro* to an almost ghost-like immateriality. But neither of these paintings is actually executed in monochrome – *Vétheuil*, for example, uses a subtle interplay of chalky lilacs, pinks, greens and blues, which evidently escaped Fauré.

At the other extreme lies Monet's exploration of warm, vibrant colour harmonies in *Autumn Effect at Argenteuil* (1873, London, Courtauld Institute Galleries). In this painting he once again abandons traditional linear and aerial perspective and defines space instead with a diminishing scale of brushstrokes and by exploiting the 'spatial' qualities of the complementary colours orange and blue – 'warm' orange appears to push towards the picture plane, its 'cool' complementary blue appears to recede. The painting also eschews the Golden Section, being divided instead roughly in half (as *La Grenouillère* had been).

On the left-hand side of the composition the division between land and water melts in a blaze of golden leaves and their reflections, vividly accented with greens, pinks and myriad other hues. The surface of the water breaks through these reflections only in the right-hand foreground, and then seems to be superimposed – anticipating the spatial ambiguities of Monet's *Waterlilies* series. This luminous dissolution of solid and liquid is intensified by Monet's physical handling of the paint. Like Degas, Monet at this time dried out his oil colours on blotting paper. But whereas Degas would dissolve the residue with turpentine, Monet retained the paint's stiff, chalky brilliance. In this painting, the thicker consistency of paint is used to echo the texture of leaves floating on the river's surface; rather more unusually, Monet animates the clump of trees on the right-hand side by scoring the surface of the paint with the handle of his brush.

As Laforgue was to articulate a decade later, the spacious academic canons of perspective and *chiaroscuro* were now overthrown by sensations rendered purely in terms of vibrant, atmospheric colour.

....
Claude MONET, Autumn Effect at Argenteuil, *1873, London, Courtauld Institute Galleries. The motif is taken from an enclosed backwater on the southern reaches of the Seine; ahead through the vista lie the main stream of the river and the distant town of Argenteuil.*
....

Katsushika HOKUSAI, Fuji seen
from Nakahara, *London, Victoria
& Albert Museum.*

He did not study long under his master, for he lost him when he was 16 years of age. Since then he did not seek another master, for he had an ambition to establish an independent school. For that purpose he studied hard by himself, and had often to climb mountains and descend to valleys, in order to sketch from Nature. Thus he established a realistic school of landscape. (Edward F. Strange, *Hiroshige's Woodblock Prints,* Dover, 1983.)

As the epitaph of the Japanese artist Ando Hiroshige (1797–1858) indicates, the rise of a naturalist landscape art during the 19th century was not an exclusively European phenomenon. Since the Tokugawa period of the 16th and 17th centuries, Japan had possessed a thriving school of genre painters and printmakers who depicted contemporary life in scenes known as *ukiyo-e* ('pictures from the floating world'). This *ukiyo-e* school reached its apogee during the late 18th and early 19th centuries with the coloured woodblock prints of Kitagawa Utamaro (1754–1806), Katsushika Hokusai [1760–1849), and Hiroshige. Executed using cherrywood blocks, which required the most sophisticated collaboration between designer, engraver, and printer, these *ukiyo-e* prints were nonetheless an essentially plebeian art form tailored to the demands of the trading classes and selling at a price equivalent to a fraction of a penny.

While Utamaro specialized in images of fashionable beauties, Hokusai and Hiroshige concentrated on landscape, particularly the environs of Mount Fuji and the great trade routes. Their new vision of landscape had been stimulated by a contemporary vogue for travel books and novels like Ikku Jippensha's *Hizakurige* of 1802. In artistic terms this vision was also vitalized by elements of European perspective acquired from topographical engravings – particularly cheap *vue d'optique* prints – which had been imported through the Dutch trading community at Nagasaki. Thus Japanese art at its most 'European' was to prove the dominant foreign influence on French Impressionist painting.

Japanese prints first became popular in Paris during the 1860s. As early as 1862, M. and Mme. Desoye – who had lived in Japan – opened *La Porte Chinoise,* a shop in the Rue de Rivoli specializing in Japanese and Chinese artefacts. It was frequented by Baudelaire, Fantin-Latour, Manet, and Whistler. As

  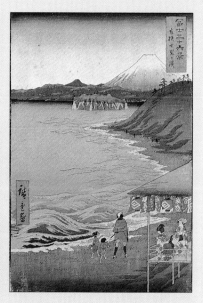

is suggested by Manet's *Portrait of Emile Zola,* Japanese prints (although still relatively expensive) had become a common sight in artistic circles by the mid 1860s. The craze for *japonisme* was given a further impetus by a Japanese pavilion at the 1867 Exposition Universelle.

Monet and Degas eventually amassed large collections of Japanese prints, mostly by Hokusai and Hiroshige. Both these French artists immediately recognized the originality of their Japanese counterparts, but whereas an artist such as Whistler exploited the Japanese art for its exotic, decorative qualities, Monet and Degas analyzed and synthesized its principles.

The cross-fertilization between Japanese and Impressionism are implicit, for example, in Hiroshige's *Spring Rain at Tsuchiyama,* from *The 53 Stations of the Tokaido* series, first published c.1833. The motif of pouring rain was exceptionally rare in Western art, but following the impact of such Japanese prints this common enough feature of the Northern European climate began to interest Degas, Pissarro, and Van Gogh. Aside from this motif, Degas' *Jockeys in the Rain* (c.1886, Glasgow, Burrell Collection) uses a characteristic range of *japoniste* elements which can be compared to Hiroshige's *Tsuchiyama.* Both artists use an 'open', asymmetrical composition which hinges on a long diagonal emphasis; both truncate figures to heighten the immediacy of the scene; both audaciously use a void for dramatic emphasis; and both use colour in broad, 'flat' expanses.

But, as might be expected from such long-distance cultural interactions, the influence of Japanese prints on Impressionism was often one of shared misconceptions. The X-shaped geometry common in the suburban vistas of Monet, Pissarro and Sisley derives ultimately from Japanese artists' rudimentary grasp of Western single-point perspective. And the vibrant colours of Japanese prints, so admired by the Impressionists, may well have been derived in turn from the lurid hand-coloured gradations of cheap 18th-century European topographical prints.

Whatever its sources, the Japanese printmaker's flair for colour and composition were an indispensible catalyst for the Impressionists' own innovations. As the critic Théodore Duret put it in his pamphlet *The Impressionist Painters of 1878:* '. . . we had to wait until the arrival of Japanese albums before anyone dared to sit down on the bank of a river to juxtapose on canvas a boldly red roof, a white wall, a green poplar, a yellow road, and blue water. Before Japan it was impossible; the painter always lied.' (Nochlin, p.8–9).

Concerning truth, we need only look at Hokusai's *Fuji from the Pass of Mishima, Kahi Province,* from *36 Views of Fuji.* As the branches of the great tree in the foreground reach down to touch the summit of sacred Mount Fuji, anticipating the pine branches 'stroking' Cézanne's *Mont Sainte-Victoire* (1885–7 Courtauld Institute Galleries), we become aware of an inheritance more profound.

QUESTIONS AND ANSWERS

*Paul CÉZANNE, The Castle at
Medan, 1880, The Burrell
Collection, Glasgow Art Gallery and
Museum. A view (which was once
owned by Gauguin) of Zola's house at
Medan where Cézanne had visited his
friend during the summer of 1880.*

As a coherent, unified movement, Impressionism was as fugitive as its visual raw materials. During the 1880s the fragmentation of the group was compounded by the struggles of each individual artist to find a way of further developing a highly successful, but ultimately limited, artistic formula.

The year 1880 can be seen as a watershed. The fourth Impressionist exhibition of the preceding year had been in financial and popular terms relatively successful. An estimated 260 works were exhibited by 15 artists (now joined by Gauguin and Degas' protégé Mary Cassatt, but without Renoir, Cézanne, Sisley and Morisot. These paintings were seen by 16,000 visitors, some of whom bought enough pictures for the exhibitors to be able to record a 439 francs profit.

One of the newer members of the independent *milieu* was Gustave Caillebotte, a highly original painter in the Realist tradition and a tireless motivator of the Impressionists who called on the artists to take courage. To several observers this is precisely what the titular leader of the Impressionists lacked when, in 1880, perhaps goaded by Renoir's success at the Salon with *Madame Charpentier,* Monet submitted two paintings to the Salon jury. They duly rejected the more important of the two, *The Ice Floes,* (1880, Vermont, Shelburne Museum), which had been painted in the studio from *plein-air* studies – a significant return to Monet's Salon-oriented procedures of the 1860s which suggested a renewed desire to create a more considered image.

Monet's 'abdication' to the Salon was seen by both artists and critics as a crippling blow to the Impressionist group identity. The ill-prepared fifth *Exposition d'Artistes Indépendants* of 1880, held at 10 Rue des Pyramides, now included only six of the original exhibitors from the first exhibition of 1874 – Caillebotte, Degas, Guillaumin, Morisot, Pissarro, Rouart – and could hardly be described as an Impressionist exhibition. Of the others, Monet, Renoir and probably Cézanne, had submitted to the Salon, while Sisley had become a semi-recluse far from Paris at Veneux-Nadon, near Moret. Thus on 2 April, 1880 (the second day of the *Indépendants* exhibition) Henry Havard of *Le Siècle* could comment: 'Moreover, let us acknowledge that Impressionism is dying. The holy phalanx is no longer up to strength. Degas is still without disciples, and Pissarro generates no pupils. In addition, the former leaders are deserting. Claude Monet has gone over to the enemy; this year he exhibits at the Salon.' (*The New Painting*, Phaidon/Oxford, 1986.)

The 1880 *Indépendants* exhibition closed on 30 April. The following June, Monet organized a one-man show at the offices of *La Vie Moderne,* a gesture which underlined the fragmentation of the Impressionist group. Fragmentation was followed by recrimination, with Degas the main culprit. A distinct breach had occurred between the core of *plein air* Impressionists from the studio Gleyre, and the 'urban' bourgeois Impressionists such as Degas and Manet (who was still relentlessly courting official recognition). This left Pissarro and Caillebotte, who were both committed to the idea of independent exhibitions, torn between allegiances. There were to be three further independent group exhibitions, but only that

....
ABOVE

Claude MONET, Rue Sainte-
Denis, Celebration of 30 June
1878, *Rouen, Musée des Beaux-Arts.*
....
OPPOSITE Claude MONET,
The Ice Floes, *1880, Paris, Musée
d'Orsay. A preliminary study for the
painting which was rejected by the
1880 Salon.*
....

A B O V E *Paul CÉZANNE,*
L'Estaque, *c.1878–79, Paris,*
Musée d'Orsay.

O P P O S I T E *Camille PISSARRO,*
La Côte des Boeufs at the
Hermitage, Pontoise, *1877,*
London, National Gallery.

of 1882 could be regarded as representative of the Impressionist ideal, and Degas was excluded from it.

A number of factors lie behind the fragmentation of the Impressionist group in the 1880s. The personal circumstances of the artists had changed, they lived in different areas, and the Paris cafés no longer served to focus their collective resolve. Since 1878, Monet had lived at Vétheuil in an extraordinary household comprising the families of the artist and his ruined former-patron, Ernest Hoschedé; Cézanne was spending more and more time at L'Estaque; Pissarro and Sisley, hounded by creditors, were forced to live semi-peripatetic lives outside Paris.

The Impressionists' lack of confidence in the independent exhibition as a means of gaining recognition was part of a more fundamental crisis of artistic purpose. The dates and degrees of this 'crisis' varied for each individual – ranging from the near-breakdown of Pissarro in the late 1870s to Monet's seemingly smooth changes of direction in the early 1880s – yet each artist was faced with the same central question: 'Where do I go from here?'. The Impressionists recognized the inherent limitations of an art based on pure sensation, but its further development proved more problematic. This was recognized by Renoir, talking in later life: 'Around 1883 a break occurred in my work. I had gone to the end of Impressionism and I was reaching the conclusion that I didn't know how either to paint or draw. In a word,

I was at a dead end.' (Rewald, p.486).

This question, and some of its answers, are implicit as early as 1877 in Pissarro's *La Côte des Boeufs at the Hermitage, Pontoise* (London, National Gallery). Painted in the same year as *Red Roofs*, and exhibited with the latter in the fourth Impressionist exhibition of 1879, *La Côte des Boeufs* suggests the reciprocal influence of Cézanne on Pissarro. Pissarro had spent part of 1877 painting side-by-side with Cèzanne and it is he who stimulated the painting's new concerns.

Unlike *Red Roofs*, *La Côte des Boeufs* is a relatively large painting which abandons the traditional horizontal format for the vertical. This in turn augments the composition's insistently vertical grid of trees which are cropped by the painting's upper edge (a motif to be later painted by Monet in his *Poplars on the Epte* series of 1891). Pissarro once again uses his favoured motif of a receding path with figures, but here the device is spatially ambiguous, 'flattened' in a dense mesh of tiny brushstrokes applied in all directions (some of which were applied in the studio).

Structured geometry, a thickly textured paint surface, and lively colour accents declare the painting as a two-dimensional, *made* thing, representing nature at another remove. Pissarro's emphasis on structure, vivified colour and painterly texture are concerns which might distinguish *La Côte des Boeufs* as (to borrow Cubism's terminology) a *synthetic* Impressionist painting, as distinct from his earlier *analytical* works.

Such had been the concerns of Cézanne during the previous summer at L'Estaque where he had painted two works for his patron Victor Chocquet. Cézanne wrote to Pissarro describing the scene:

. . . it is like a playing card, red roofs against the blue sea. If the weather is favourable, I shall perhaps carry them (i.e. the pictures for Chocquet) through to the end. Up to the present I have done nothing. Motifs can be found here which would require up to three or four months work, and that is possible because the vegetation doesn't change. It is composed of olive and pine trees which always preserve their foliage. The sun is so terrific that it seems to me as if the objects were silhouetted not only in black and white, but in blue, red, brown, and violet. I may be mistaken, but this seems to me to be the opposite of modelling.

Cézanne's burgeoning synthetic vision was re-evaluating the role of both form and colour in a painting. In his landscapes of the later 1870s nature becomes increasingly controlled by a harmonious, geometrical 'architecture'; solidly modelled forms are played off against great flattening expanses of sea: space is realized through the interaction of 'warm and 'cool' colours, and solids through the localized interplay of colour applied in modulated tints. The inspiration for this new synthesis lay in Cézanne's recognition that he could not 'reproduce' nature – 'it must be represented by something else . . . by colour'.

The desire for a balance between the solidity of natural forms and the flatness of the painted canvas, impelled Cézanne to explore every available means of unifying his compositions. Uniformity of brushwork was one such means, and by the end of the 1870s Cézanne had begun to deploy the so-called 'constructive' brushstroke – paint applied in units of consistent scale, shape, and direction (a technique made easier by the introduction of tin ferrules on brushes earlier in the century). In *The Castle at Medan* (1880, Glasgow, Burrell Museum), natural and man-made forms are relentlessly ordered parallel to the picture plane, but this effect is softened by regulated oblong brushstrokes arranged in diagonal hatchings; in addition to unifying the composition, they suggest the vibrant movements of river, trees, and sky.

Cézanne's determination to endow his subjects with a unified structure led to a continued preoccupation with still life, a genre which allowed him a free hand to re-order the motif without compromising his truth to nature. The still lifes of this period continue to be based, ultimately, on the 18th-century tradition of Chardin, but now the objects have the intensely solid, monumental forms of Cézanne's renewed vision of nature.

Cézanne's work of the late 1870s and early 80s was only one, albeit far-reaching, answer to the question raised by Impressionism. Monet, Pissarro, Renoir, Sisley each found their own solution to the Impressionist stylistic *impasse*, and two recurrent themes can be traced through this latter 'synthetic' phase of Impressionism: the intensification of often densely applied colour, and the enlargement of forms.

In the case of an artist as single-minded as Monet, the Impressionists' 'crisis' was manifested in a shift in direction, an amplication, rather than any paralyzing loss of confidence. In the 1870s Monet had worked

....
R I G H T Edgar DEGAS, The Little Dancer of Fourteen, *London, Tate Gallery. A bronze version of the wax original exhibited in the sixth Impressionist exhibition of 1881 and now in the Mr and Mrs Paul Mellon Collection, Upperville, Virginia. The model was Marie Van Goethen, a Belgian girl who was a ballet pupil at the Paris Opera.*
....
O P P O S I T E Edgar DEGAS, After the Bath: Woman Drying Herself, *c.1880s–90s, pastel on paper, London, National Gallery.*
....

mainly in the Seine valley, but during the following decade he travelled further afield to Normandy, Brittany and the south, in search of more extreme natural effects. His own synthesis can be seen at its most dramatic in *Varengeville Church* (1882, Birmingham, Barber Institute of Fine Arts), where a 'Japanese' design, luxuriant colour, and monumental natural forms are combined to capture the gorgeous atmosphere of a cliff-top sunset near Dieppe. The painting is notable for its thorough application of Japanese design principles: the 'open' asymmetrical composition with its high horizon, steeply raked intersecting diagonals, and abrupt transitions of tone are all compositional trade-marks of Hiroshige (1797–1858). As was the case with Cézanne's landscapes, the scene is conceived using colours – applied in two distinct stages – which *represent* rather than *reproduce* those in nature. Colour relationships became of overriding importance for Monet.

While Monet's expressive application of colour is closely reflected in the later works of Sisley – although tinged with a desolate sense of *tristesse* – his grand natural and man-made motifs are echoed more indirectly in other Impressionists' renewed enthusiasm for the large-scale figure. This took a variety of forms. In the case of Degas, the search for solidity and structure found literal expression in sculptures such as *The Little Dancer* (c. 1881, versions in the Musée d'Orsay, the Shelburne Museum, Vermont, and the Tate Gallery). This work – typically for the latter stages of Degas' career – was created using mixed media, and was exhibited at the sixth Impressionist exhibition of 1881. Significantly, Degas' first exploration of sculpture as a medium coincided with Rodin's use of broken, 'impressionistic' modelling to animate surfaces and suggest internal masses. From the 1880s onwards the single figure, particularly the candidly observed nude woman at her *toilette*, began to dominate Degas' pictorial imagery. With Degas' eyesight deteriorating, this seemingly limitless procession of the female body caught in every conceivable pose is distinguished by its broad, expressive handling of pastel, fusing the techniques of drawing and painting.

Degas was perhaps also instrumental in resolving the agonizing doubts that had afflicted Pissarro from around 1877. In 1880 Pissarro collaborated with Degas on a series of prints intended for a journal to be called *Le Jour et la Nuit*. A combination of Degas' proximity and the absence of *plein air* landscape motifs while working on these prints resulted in

Pissarro turning to the figure for his canvases. Although he vigorously denied it, his chosen figure-type of the peasant was presumed by critics to have been derived from Millet. However, the two artists' respective treatments of this common subject could not have been more dissimilar: Millet's grandiloquent images of impoverished peasant labour contrast diametrically with Pissarro's diffusely handled, idyllic vision of peasant recreation.

During the 1880s, figure compositions continued to pour from the studios of Renoir and Manet, both of whom had been enjoying considerable success as society portrait painters. *Luncheon of the Boating Party* (1880–81, Washington, Phillips Collection) is probably the most famous example of Renoir's talent for pictorial charm. However, feeling a loss of direction in the early 1880s he travelled widely through Europe in search of classicizing inspiration from such masters as Raphael, Velasquez, and Rubens. The resultant, sharply contoured, stylization of Renoir's *The Bathers* (1885–7, Philadelphia Museum of Art), based on a fountain relief at Versailles, was the very antithesis of Impressionism.

In contrast, Manet, after a succession of facile society portraits, tantalizingly recaptured the expressive power of his early works in *A Bar at the Folies-Bergère* (1881–82, London, Courtauld Galleries), exhibited at the Salon less than a year before his death on 30 April, 1883. The scene is the bar of an electrically lit café-concert; an impassive barmaid gazes outwards at the implied viewer whose reflection appears on the right of the composition. The Folies-Bergère was a well-known haunt of prostitutes and their clients. Manet's art had come full circle, compromising the male Salon-goer as much as he had been two decades previously by the notorious *Olympia*.

During the mid-1880s there arrived on the Parisian art scene a new generation of young painters who were to question the fundamental premises of Impressionism. In the vanguard was Georges Seurat (1859–91), a former student at the Ecole des Beaux-

OPPOSITE Camille PISSARRO, The Shepherdess, Peasant girl with a Stick, *1881, Paris, Musée d'Orsay. Included among over 30 works shown by Pissarro at the 1882 seventh Impressionist exhibition.*

Arts under Heinrich Lehmann, whose *Bathers at Asnières* – painted at the age of 24 – was an astonishingly mature *critique* and revitalization of the Impressionist tradition.

Exhibited during the spring of 1884 in the canteen of the Salon des Indépendants, *Bathers at Asnières* (1883–4, London, National Gallery) was Seurat's first large-scale oil painting. He had previously undergone a rigorous self-imposed apprenticeship, immersing himself in books on the theory of colour and vision, such as Ogden Rood's *Modern Chromatics* (French translation published 1881) and Chevreul's *Law of Simultaneous Contrast of Colours* (published 1839); he had made a specific study of Delacroix's paintings, particularly the murals at Saint Sulpice; he had made numerous *plein air* oil studies using his own 'constructive' brushstroke, confronting the banal realities of the Paris suburb, the *banlieue;* and he had perfected the art of modulating tone in a series of Conté crayon drawings which placed him in the first rank of draughtsmen from any era.

These methodical procedures were continued in the making of *Bathers at Asnières.* The general arrangement of the composition has been traced back to Puvis de Chavannes (1824–98) and Poussin, particularly the latter's *Finding of Moses* of 1638, which was in the Louvre. However, these compositions were only a preliminary means of organizing his motif, which was then relentlessly observed in the open air and re-arranged in the studio within a series of some 24 (surviving) painted and drawn sketches. Seurat devoted particular attention to the two main figures seated on the river bank, finalizing their poses by drawing the live model in the studio. These individual studies were also used to experiment with the effects of simultaneous contrast – in this case, the juxtaposition of tonal extremes – which gives the forms such tremendous solidity.

The scene is the west bank of the Seine at Asnières, one of several industrial 'suburb-towns' which had sprung up outside Paris from the 1860s onwards. In the distance lie the factories of Clichy; to the right, La Grande Jatte, an island inundated by Sunday trippers, which was to be immortalized in Seurat's next major

....
Pierre-Auguste RENOIR,
Luncheon of the Boating Party,
1880–81, Washington, Phillips
Collection.
....

composition. The time is the afternoon of a mid-summer weekend. Boys and workers in various stages of undress relax in the enervating heat; three of them keep cool by dipping into the river (which in reality was at that point uncomfortably close to the main Paris sewage works).

Seurat was known to have left-wing sympathies, and the picture can be read on one level as an immensely dignified image of the Parisian dispossessed, gazing vacantly towards the bourgeois, Haussmannized city which at once uses, and rejects them. On another level, it is simply a picture about heat. The *Bather's* large scale, total studio execution, and austere, static interplay of the dominant horizontal with diagonals and verticals (which in the background results in contradictory wind directions) might seem opposed to the Impressionist credo – but it is nonetheless an intensely realistic evocation of a hot summer's day.

Seurat used a number of techniques to achieve this 'intensified' effect. The canvas has a thick white ground which lends it an overall blond tonality; 'fringes' of extreme light and dark tones solidify the figures with simultaneous contrasts; a red shadow is cast from the right-hand bather's hat, enlivening the green of the grass bank behind him; and most significantly of all, the green grass is intensified throughout using criss-crossed flecks of complementary colours. Seurat disposed these flecks with the aid of a colour wheel, a device previously employed by Delacroix, Chevreul, and Rood. This allowed him to determine the precise complementary of the tints he derived from his primary colours: ie varieties of orange (which combine the primaries red and yellow) would be juxtaposed with tints of its complementary, blue.

The application of this system was comparatively informal in *Bathers at Asnières*. As in Impressionist painting, the colours were intended to vibrate in the observer's eye through their proximity; but from the mid 1880s onwards the continuous refinement of this system led Seurat to evolve a technique he termed 'chromo-luminarism' – otherwise known as divisionism – in which dense networks of coloured 'dots' create

the effect of tonal transitions when mixed by the eye.

Seurat, however, had not fully codified his chromo-luminarist system when he embarked on what was to be the masterwork of the Neo-Impressionist move-ment – *Sunday Afternoon on the Island of La Grande Jatte* (1884–6, Chicago Institute of Arts). Originally in-tended for the abortive 1885 Salon des Indépendants,

....
Georges SEURAT, The Gleaner, Conté crayon, c.1883, London, British Museum. Seurat here pays an obvious debt to the great mid-19th-century painter of peasant life, Jean-Francois Millet (1814–75).
....

this colossal painting eventually became the centre-piece of an eighth Impressionist exhibition in 1886 which was largely given over to the Neo-Impressionist aesthetic. In addition to the nine works exhibited by Seurat, a further 18 were exhibited by his disciple Paul Signac (1863–1935) as well as works by Pissarro in a newly acquired divisionist idiom. *La Grande Jatte* is an epic synthesis of Impressionist brushwork and divisionist reworkings, naturalistic observation and hieratic stylization, visual jokes and straight-laced *gravitas*, poetry and science, which offers a limitless range of interpretation for each succeeding generation. Seurat tended to regard the work-in-progress as a unified whole, and there is a haunting contrast between his uninhabited preparatory studies and the teeming humanity in the finished painting.

Impressionism, even at its most 'synthetic' in the later paintings of Monet, Cézanne and Seurat, continued to cling to the ideal of truth to observed nature. When this ideological bedrock was questioned, and answered in a number of different ways, the Post-Impressionist movement began to stir.

This new aesthetic was largely the achievement of Paul Gauguin (1848–1903) and Vincent Van Gogh (1853–90) during the later 1880s. The narrative of the two artists' lives and their brief friendship – culminating in their violent estrangement at Arles in December 1888, Van Gogh's breakdown and eventual suicide two years later, and Gauguin's defection to the South Seas – is a saga too well embedded in the popular mythology of art to bear repetition here. However, the outlines of the relationship between their art and the Impressionists are worth discussing.

Gauguin and Van Gogh had much in common. Both artists had come to painting late in life after initially pursuing 'careers' (Gauguin as a stockbroker, Van Gogh as a missionary); both seized on painting as the exclusive means of endowing their lives with purpose; both received little formal training, which preserved their independence of vision but at times made them appear to be 'amateur' painters; both were emancipated by their exposure to Impressionism; but both looked to their own, subjective responses for a central dynamic.

Gauguin's earliest works were in a Barbizon-derived idiom (as indeed were Van Gogh's) until Pissarro once again played a pivotal role in the artist's career by becoming his mentor in about 1876. In contrast to an artist such as Seurat, there was a lengthy gestation period before the emergence of Gauguin's individual voice. His *The Edge of the Wood* of 1885 (Otterloo, Kröller-Müller Museum), for example, could at first glance be taken for a Pissarro of the same period – that is until one notices that the trees are being moved by forces more powerful than the wind, or even the artist's own 'personal style'.

Van Gogh arrived in Paris the following year, in 1886. After an initially lukewarm response to Impressionist painting, he rapidly adopted some of its technical procedures, such as a generally lighter palette and small-scale, broken brushwork. Yet even in the early Parisian work, *Le Moulin de la Galette, Montmartre* (1886, Glasgow City Art Gallery), violent emotions are evident, constricted within the Impres-

Paul GAUGUIN, Vision after the Sermon, *1888, Edinburgh, National Gallery of Scotland. A pivotal image in the early history of Post-Impressionism created – from the point of view of both the artist and the peasant women in the painting – entirely from the imagination.*

sionist idiom. In fact Van Gogh was to use Impressionism highly selectively, turning instead to the more personally expressive values of Delacroix (whose works he copied while in the asylum at St-Rémy in 1889–90).

Van Gogh and Gauguin met for the first time in Paris in 1886. Collectively and individually they had become increasingly aware of what they perceived as Impressionism's intellectual and emotional limitations, its essentially *passive* responses to the exterior world.

In 1885 Gauguin had put forward an alternative direction in a letter to his former stockbroker and colleague Emile Schuffenecker, who had also taken

Paul GAUGUIN, Self Portrait
with a Palette, *Los Angeles, 1893,*
Norton Simon Foundation.

....
Vincent VAN GOGH, Self Portrait
with Bandaged Ear, 1889,
London, Courtauld Institute
....

up painting: 'Go on working, *freely and furiously*, you will make progress and sooner or later your worth will be recognized, if you have any. Above all, don't perspire over a picture. A strong emotion can be translated immediately: dream on it and seek its simplest form.' (Nochlin, p.159.)

This primacy of the artist's emotion and imagination, and their visualization using simplified forms and symbolic colours was first achieved by Gauguin three years later in his *Vision After the Sermon* (1888, Edinburgh, National Gallery of Scotland). A key work in the history of Post-Impressionism, this scene of Breton peasant women was inspired by a slightly earlier composition on a similar theme by Emile Bernard (1868–1941). Fortunately a letter survives from 1888 in which Gauguin describes the painting to Van Gogh:

I believe that I have achieved a great rustic, superstitious simplicity in these figures. Everything is very severe. The cow under the tree is very small relative to reality, and . . . for me, in this painting, the landscape and the struggle exist only within the imagination of the praying people, the product of the sermon. This is why there is a contrast between the 'real' people and the struggle in its landscape devoid of naturalism and out of proportion. (J. Rewald, *Post-Impressionism*, 1978.)

Gauguin omitted, however, to mention the all-important source which distinguished this painting from its Impressionistic predecessors – the artist's own imagination. Gauguin was eventually to call this subjective, anti-naturalistic approach *synthetism*.

Van Gogh by this time was also leaving Impressionism behind, and from Arles in 1888 he wrote to his brother Theo:

. . . I should not be surprised if the impressionists soon find fault with my way of working, for it has been fertilized by the ideas of Delacroix rather than by theirs. Because, instead of trying to reproduce exactly what I see before my eyes, I use colour more arbitrarily to express myself forcibly. (Rewald, *Post-Impressionism*, 1978.)

The force of Van Gogh's terrible expression compelled him to transmogrify nature itself, to create images in which every line, shape, and patch of colour are an equivalent of an emotion.

The Symbolist painter Odilon Redon had prophesized when reviewing the 1880 Impressionist exhibition, 'the future belongs to the subjective world'.

....
Vincent VAN GOGH, A Cornfield
with Cypresses, *1889, London,*
National Gallery.
....

DELACROIX

Eugène Delacroix, Sea at Dieppe,
1852, Paris, Louvre.

One of the few elements to unite Impressionism, Neo-Impressionism, and Post-Impressionism was the varied inspiration each drew from the life and art of Eugène Delacroix (1798–1863). The uncompromising integrity of this great Romantic's artistic credo, his contempt for the academic establishment, and his far-reaching, painterly innovations, were a presiding, formative example for a generation of radical French painters. Degas, Monet, Renoir, Cézanne, Seurat and Van Gogh were all known to have studied Delacroix's work in detail. Cézanne – who in the 1860s made a copy of Delacroix's *Barque of Dante* (1822, Louvre) and who owned a watercolour by him of *Flowers* (c. 1849, Louvre) – even went as far as to plan an *Apotheosis of Delacroix* only a decade before his own death in 1906.

Delacroix was a different artist's artist to every individual and every faction of the later 19th-century French avant-garde. The Impressionists turned to Delacroix in his guise as the pre-eminent colourist of the French tradition, as an observer of nature, and as an audacious manipulator of paint who renounced finish in the search for overall pictorial unity. His use of colour and its anticipation of Impressionist practices has been much discussed, but some key anticipations stand out.

At a relatively early date in his career Delacroix was painting coloured shadows (as did Pre-Raphaelite landscape painters such as Ford Madox Brown in the 1850s), but his perceptions of light and colour went beyond this simple natural observation. For example, he would often tint the shadow cast by a coloured mass with its complementary, rather than the colour itself – a phenomenon analyzed in nature by the influential chemist Michel Chevreul (1786–1889). Colour masses would also take an even more positive role by emanating reflections throughout the composition. Some of this sensitivity to light and colour can be gauged in an entry in Delacroix's *Journals*, Monet's favourite book in the twilight of his last years. In an entry for 7 September, 1856, Delacroix described an urchin he had seen climbing up the foun-

tain in the Place Saint-Sulpice in full sunlight: '... dull orange in the lights, the most brilliant violets for the transitional passages into shadow, and golden reflections in the shadows thrown up from the ground. The orange and violet were alternately predominant or else mixed together. The golden tint had some green in it.'

Delacroix was also admired by the Impressionists as a painter of nature. He executed no *plein air* canvases, but his landscape studies executed both in the open air and from memory note acutely the interactions of light, land, sea, and colour. Monet eventually owned some of these studies, and a precursor for his *Impression: Sunrise* can be found in a Delacroix study such as the broadly treated *Sea at Dieppe* [1852, Paris, Ex Collection Beurdeley, (courtesy Raymond Laniepce, Paris)].

For the Post-Impressionist movement Delacroix was yet another artist. Van Gogh in particular looked to him as a means of breaking away from Impressionist practices, concentrating instead on Delacroix's use of colour to convey emotional values. In common with Van Gogh, Delacroix believed in the primacy of the individual imagination over what he felt were specious notions of artistic 'realism', and like Van Gogh he used paintings as metaphors, as outward expressions of an intensely personal search for meaning in life and art. Among Delacroix's most poignant works in this vein is *Ovid Among the Scythians* (c.1855–59, London, National Gallery). The subject is the banishment in AD 8 of the Emperor Augustus' court poet to Tomis on the Black Sea coast. Delacroix has taken the desolation of the poet's exile as a metaphor for his own estrangement from the artistic establishment, indeed from bourgeois Parisian society as a whole. The 19-year-old Monet saw this painting at the 1859 Salon and described it in a letter to Boudin as – ironically enough – 'no more than indications, sketches, but as ever full of life and movement'. Looking foward to Monet's own mature works, these words aptly convey Delacroix's affinity with the Impressionists.

CHAPTER SIX

THE LEGACY

Paul CÉZANNE, Still Life with a
Basket, *c.1888–90, Paris, Musée
d'Orsay.*

issemination, as much as fragmentation, was the story of Impressionism during the 1880s, and by the end of the decade the movement was no longer an exclusively Fench phenomenon. Paris continued to attract a large number of artists from Europe and North America, gravitating to the city that was the art centre, and market of the world. Most of these foreign artists were drawn to Paris for its academic training rather than its Impressionist avant-garde. Many of the more independently minded visitors found the Post-Impressionist developments of Seurat, Signac, Gauguin, and Van Gogh a greater stimulus than Impressionist 'naturalism' which, by the late 1880s, had seemingly become outmoded. The result was that Impressionism established kindred, coherent movements in only two other countries – America and England. In both cases the adoption of the Impressionist aesthetic was selective and problematic.

America was conspicuous in being sympathetic towards Impressionism at an early date, in marked contrast to England where, during the 1870s, no fewer than ten exhibitions at Durand-Ruel's Bond Street Galleries had met with supercilious indifference. Some of this American open-mindedness can be put down to the groundwork achieved by Mary Cassatt in France (1844–1926). Born in Pittsburgh, the daughter of a banker, Mary Cassatt studied extensively in Europe before settling permanently in Paris in 1873. The following year she exhibited at the Salon, where her *Portrait of Mme. Cortier* (1874, Private Collection) was favourably noticed by Degas. In 1877 she met Degas himself, becoming one of the few women to gain the friendship and respect of this cantankerous misogynist. Degas invited Cassatt to exhibit with the Impressionists, and his *protégé* duly contributed to their shows in 1879, 1880, 1881, and 1886.

Cassatt's tautly composed, but fluently executed, paintings are remarkable for their empathetic inter-

pretations of the bond between mother and child, particularly in view (or perhaps because) of Cassatt's own childlessness. The static, often linear, emphasis of her work gives it a further individuality within the Impressionist *oeuvre*.

Mary Cassatt might have been expected to play a pivotal role in the introduction of Impressionism to America, but she remained in France and did not revisit America until 1898. She nevertheless exerted considerable influence over American collectors visiting France; for example, in 1875 she persuaded the future Louisine Havermeyer to purchaser Degas' gouache and pastel of the preceding year, the *Ballet Rehearsal*, (Kansas City, Nelson-Atkins Museum). This seems to have been the first Impressionist work to have been publicly exhibited in America when it was put on show at the American Watercolour Society in 1878.

It was to be during the later 1870s and early 80s that America began to familiarize itself with the Impressionist world. In 1879, Manet's *Execution of Maximilian* was exhibited in New York and Boston, receiving a surprisingly positive response from the New York critics. This was followed in the autumn of 1883 by a further exhibition in Boston mounted by the Foreign Exhibition Association, which included Impressionist paintings from Durand-Ruel's stock. By the end of the decade, the Metropolitan Museum of Art had acquired Manet's *Child with a Sword* (1860) and *Woman with a Parrot* (1866), in conspicuous contrast to the indifference of England's public collections.

However, the most important event in the early history of Impressionism in America was Durand-Ruel's momentous exhibition held in New York during the spring of 1886. This first comprehensive selection of Impressionist paintings to be seen in America – including 23 works by Degas, 17 by Manet, 15 by Sisley, 7 by Morisot, 38 by Renoir, 42 by Pissarro, 48 by Monet (but oddly, none by Cassatt) – opened at the American Art Association, New York on 10 April under the title of *A Special Exhibition of Works in Oil and Pastel by The Impressionists of Paris*. The show created such a stir that it transferred to the National Academy of Design – an important bastion of the American artistic establishment – where it reopened on 25 May.

The reviewers' opinions were inevitably mixed, but were on balance favourable. A positive reaction also came from American collectors, a few of whom, such as the New Yorker Erwin Davis, had already bought Impressionist works. Seven or eight paintings

Childe HASSAM, Celia Thaxter in her Garden,
*1892, Gift of John Gellatly, National Museum of
American Art, Smithsonian Institution.*

were sold within the first two weeks, and Durand-Ruel was reported to have eventually earned a total $40,000 from the exhibition. Such was the unexpected success of this exhibition that the following year rival New York dealers attempted to use an injunction to prevent Durand-Ruel holding a second exhibition at the National Academy of Design.

As artistic circles in New York and Boston considered the significance of the Impressionst paintings they had seen, American artists in France were coming into contact with the Impressionist painters themselves. The main focus of attention – much to his exasperation – was Monet, who in 1883 had moved from Vétheuil to Giverny, a village overlooking water meadows near the Seine, about 50 miles (80km) north-west of Paris. Together with the combined Monet/Hoschedé families, the ageing painter was to

live here for the rest of his life, eventually marrying Alice Hoschedé in 1892, a year after her first husband's death. The vanguard of the American presence in Giverny had been represented by John Singer Sargent (1856–1925), an artist who experimented with Impressionist brushwork during the formative years of his career in France, and who regularly visited Monet in the later 1880s before pursuing a successful career as a virtuoso portrait painter in England and America.

....
Theodore ROBINSON, The
Wedding March, *1892, Daniel J.
Terra Collection, Terra Museum of
American Art, Chicago.*
....

The establishment of an American 'colony' at Giverny seems to date from around 1887, by which time the painters Willard Metcalf (1858–1925), Louis Ritter (1854–92), John Leslie Breck (1860–99), Theodore Robinson (1852–96), and Theodore Wendel (1857–1932) were all established in the village. Not all these painters had arrived in the village to pay homage to the founder of Impressionism – Breck later recounted that he, Robinson and Wendel had picked Giverny at random from a list of destinations in St Lazare station.

The most significant of the American 'Givernois' painters was Theodore Robinson. Born in Vermont and trained in Chicago, he had studied under Jean-Léon Gérôme in Paris in 1876 before arriving in Giverny in 1887. He was to become a close friend of Monet – as was another American artist, Lilla Cabot Perry (c.1848–1933).

Robinson inevitably came under the master's influence, loosening his early 'Salon style' with a lighter, fragmentary handling of the brush, painting out of doors, and depicting the same motif under different climatic conditions. However, in common with most American artists of the period, the pull of their own traditions of topographical realism – represented by masters such as Winslow Homer (1836–1910) and Thomas Eakins (1844–1916) (who had also studied under Gérôme) – curtailed the complete transformation of Robinson's approach. Natural observation remains paramount, but not through the concentration on transient personal sensations notated in terms of pure colour. Nonetheless, towards the end of his sojourn at Giverny, Robinson was executing paintings of considerable spontaneity and compositional originality.

Within five years the American presence in Giverny had swelled into an invasion force, the village overrun with artists eager to learn the 'secret' of Monet's art by watching him paint in the open air. This influx of admirers inevitably resulted in Monet closing his doors to all but his most valued friends.

On Theodore Robinson's return in 1892, America had a significant number of painters working in the Impressionist idiom. Six years later this school was to be formally recognized by the formation of the 'Ten American Painters' which held its first exhibition at Durand-Ruel, New York, in 1898. Although this group certainly represented the American Impressionist establishment – including Metcalf, John Twachtman (1853–1902), Childe Hassam (1859–1935), and J. Alden Weir (1852–1919) – its formation owed less to shared ideologies than to the straightforward desire to ensure optimum exhibiting conditions for their work.

Probably the most gifted of the 'Ten' was Childe Hassam, a painter who had first worked in Boston, where he gained a reputation as a magazine and newspaper illustrator. His art took a radically new direction during a second period in Paris from 1886–9, when he enrolled at the Académie Julian, exhibited at the Salon, and painted – initially at least – scenes of rainy streets reminiscent of Caillebotte. Although Hassam does not seem to have made the statutory pilgrimage to Giverny, he may well have seen Durand-Ruel's 1886 New York exhibition and Monet's retrospective exhibition at Petit's Gallery in Paris in 1889. Whatever the stimulae, Hassam's palette changed towards the end of the 1880s, rejecting what he was to call 'the molasses and bitumen school' for a more vibrant, colouristic realization of the city streets.

Hassam came closest to the ideals of French Impressionism in the first few years after his return to America in 1890 when he painted urban motifs, sometimes from a high viewpoint, in varying weather conditions. These compositions derived ultimately from the example of Monet's *Boulevard des Capucines*. Hassam also executed *plein air* landscapes during summers spent on the island of Appledore, off the New England Coast; these were vivid mosaics of touches of pure colour executed with the brush in a manner reminiscent of Monet in the 1880s.

As in France, *plein air* landscape painting was American Impressionism's preferred medium (their interior, figurative treatments being notably unadventurous by comparison). The most celebrated open-air practitioner was William Merritt Chase (1849–1916), an Indiana-born New York painter, who in 1891 founded the Shinnecock Summer Art School on Long Island. The school was enormously successful, running for 12 seasons, and his *plein air* teaching was continued at summer classes in various European cities from 1903–13.

Chase's own work sums up the extent to which the new American painting of the 1880s and 90s can be termed Impressionist according to the principles of their great French predecessors. They were executed in the open air; they depict affluent city-dwellers at leisure beside the sea; they use a bright palette of primary colours and their complementaries; the paint is applied in fragmented expanses of small strokes, often with vivid colour accents. All these conform to what we might identify as the characteristics of a painting by Monet or Renoir. Yet the lighting and climatic effects in Chase's paintings tend to be generalized, and there is little movement to imply a fleeting moment. The Impressionistic description of the motif predominates rather than – as in a Monet or Renoir – the artist's own momentary sensations. Still rooted in the compositional traditions of earlier 19th-century topographical realism, American Impressionism is a different way of painting, but not a different way of seeing.

In contrast to America, the impact of Impressionism in England was fragmentary and short-lived. In 1871 Pissarro had complained that in London there was no art, just business. This climate of establishment indifference to Impressionism culminated in 1906 when Durand-Ruel mounted at the Grafton Galleries what was arguably the greatest ever single Impressionist selling exhibition, including Renoir's *The Luncheon of the Boating Party*, *La Loge*, and Monet's *Ice Floes*. Not a single painting was sold during the exhibition.

One of the few artists in England to champion the Impressionists was the American, James McNeill Whistler (1834–1903). Trained – like Monet, Renoir and Sisley – in Gleyre's studio, Whistler settled in London in 1859, but frequently visited Paris, which kept him in contact with the leading exponents of the French avant-garde. His *White Girl* (1862) was exhibited with Manet's *Le Déjeuner sur l'Herbe* at the 1863 Salon des Refusés, and he became close friends with

both Mallarmé and Monet in the later 1880s. Although heavily influenced by Japanese art, Whistler's own highly original paintings could hardly be described as Impressionist in their provocative aestheticism, studio execution, and emphasis on meticulously worked tonal modulations. However, in his role as a cosmopolitan focal-point for young English artists, Whistler was an important propagandist for the Impressionist movement. Two young artists in particular from the Whistler circle were to paint in what could be described as an English Impressionist idiom – Walter Sickert and Philip Wilson Steer, both of whom, coincidentally, were born in 1860 and died in 1942.

Sickert's mentor was Degas, whom he described as perhaps the greatest painter the world had ever seen, and whom he met for the first time in Paris in 1883. On his return to London Sickert explained to the Whistler circle Degas' ideas that the composition should be arranged as 'if looking through a key-hole'. Sickert gave this voyeurist stance an added charge by

James Abbott McNeill WHISTLER,
Nocturne: Grey and Gold –
Westminster Bridge, *c.1871–74,*
Burrell Collection, Glasgow Art
Gallery and Museum.

O P P O S I T E *Edgar DEGAS,* Two
Dancers, *c.1895, Private*
Collection.

concentrating his modern subject matter on scenes of London's bed-sit prostitutes and their working-class clients. In common with Degas, Sickert looked to the music hall and the female nude for his motifs, later in his career often painting from photographs; but unlike Degas, Sickert's is a static world in which the sheer drabness of Edwardian London is realized by atmospheric encrustations of 'broken' impasto.

Sickert also played a key role in securing the New English Art Club as a venue to exhibit the work of the 'London Impressionists'. The New English Art Club had been founded in 1886 by French-trained artists as an alternative to the Royal Academy; in April 1888,

with Sickert on the committee, the N.E.A.C. showed Degas' *Green Dancer* and *A Summer's Evening* by Philip Wilson Steer (1887–8, Private Collection, but sold Sotheby's, 15 December, 1971, lot no. 22). Steer, having studied under Adolphe Bouguereau (1825–1905) and Cabanel (1823–89) in Paris, from 1882–84, was one of the founder members of the Club, and his painting was immediately recognized as the most monumental of early English Impressionist works.

Although Steer seems to have had little personal contact with the French Impressionists, his manner from the late 1880s to 90s is a luminous synthesis of Monet and Neo-Impressionism applied to scenes of young girls at the seaside. Perhaps more than any other foreign painter, Steer comes closest to the true ideals of the French Impressionists, rendering movement in atmosphere with a prismatic palette and 'non-descriptive' brushwork. His seaside motifs also prophetically capture the mood of the Balbec sequences in that great monument of French literary Impressionism, Proust's *A la recherche du temps perdu* (1913–27).

The London Impressionists (bolstered by the presence of Théodore Roussel and Sidney Starr) held an inaugural group exhibtion at the Goupil Gallery in 1889, but it was to last barely a decade as a recognizable movement. In the late 1890s Steer abandoned his Impressionist manner for a more traditional, Constable-derived English style, and Sickert was spending an increasing proportion of his time abroad. The New English Art Club, once the launch-pad of the most radical trends in English art, reverted to the more respectable past.

As Impressionism sent out ever-diminishing tremors of influence abroad, the artists at its epi-centre achieved their grandiloquent final resolutions.

For Monet, the year 1890 saw the emergence of a momentous new procedure – the serial paintings, which began with the *Grain Stacks* (1890–91), *Poplars on the Epte* (1891), and *Rouen Cathedral* (1892–3), finally culminating in the famous *Waterlilies* series which he worked on from c.1898 until his death in 1926. By using a series of paintings in which the same motif appeared in varying atmospheric conditions, Monet was finally able to overcome the Impressionists' disparity between sensation and execution; furthermore, when viewed together (Monet was by now well established enough to command exhibition space) the series would give the illusion of a motif in continuous atmospheric flux.

Although accounts vary, it appears that one specific experience was the catalyst behind this new direction in Monet's art. During the summer of 1890, Monet had been working in the open air painting the grain stacks in the *clos Morin*, a field lying immediately west of his house at Giverny. Certain rapidly changing atmospheric conditions arose – probably the sun breaking through mist – which required him to start canvas after canvas in quick succession in order to capture each evanescent effect.

An exhibition of the *Grain Stacks* opened at Durand-Ruel on 4 May, 1891 and included 15 paintings of the *Grain Stacks* (supplemented by a further seven miscellaneous works). It was favourably received by both critics and public, the pictures selling within a few days for prices ranging from 3,000 to 4,000 francs.

Monet at this time confided to Theodore Robinson that he wished his work to acquire 'more serious qualities'. In practical terms this resulted in him devoting more and more time to the refinement of his paintings in the studio. In formal terms it resulted in an ever-increasing concentration on the *enveloppe* (the same light diffusing over everything) and reflections, the twin obsessions of Monet's later years which both suggest the atmosphere around the motif rather than the motif itself.

Monet's final statement on this theme was the great *Waterlilies* series of c.1898-1925. Here his painting had come full circle, returning to the effects of water reflections which had preoccupied him some 30 years previously at La Grenouillère.

With subconscious motives similar to those lying behind Cézanne's preference for still life, Monet had arranged nature to his requirements by creating an elaborate water garden in a stretch of land which he had bought in 1893 below his house at Giverny. Monet maintained that the garden had been initially cultivated only for pleasure, but 'then, suddenly, I had the revelation of the magic of my pond'. A series of 10 waterscapes (c.1895–1900) incorporating the arc of the Japanese bridge were subsequently exhibited by Durand-Ruel in 1900, and a further 48 individual canvases of the *Waterlilies* at Durand-Ruel in 1909. It was around 1898 that Monet began to visualize a scheme in which monumental waterscapes would form a continuous frieze around a room, surrounding the viewer with 'the illusion of an endless whole, of water without horizon or shore' and offering 'a refuge of peaceful meditation in the midst of a

Phillip Wilson STEER, Children at the Seaside, Walberswick, *1894, Cambridge, Fitzwilliam Museum.*

flowering aquarium'.

This Herculean project, painted entirely in the studio from the memory and imagination, occupied Monet almost until his death in 1926. His struggles against old age, the fear of approaching blindness, and the tragedy of his wife's death in 1911 were matched by the tortuous frustrations of the paintings themselves, many of which were comprehensively repainted or else destroyed. Yet with the aid of continual encouragement of the French premiere Georges Clemenceau and a successful eye operation in 1923, Monet was able to complete the last of the panels in 1825. He donated two of the friezes to the French nation in commemoration of their victory in the First World War, and these remain in their specially prepared galleries at the Orangerie, Paris; the other friezes have found their way into museums and private collections elsewhere in France, Switzerland, America and England.

Monet's *Waterlilies* are the final, mystical distillations of a lifetime's realization of nature. All but the vestiges of naturalistic description have been left behind. The notional 'surface' of the pond is indicated by a few strategically placed lily pads, but this is otherwise dissolved in an ethereal liquefaction of coloured reflections and mist which is in turn animated and made spatially ambiguous by the interaction of complementaries and the mobility of warm versus cool colours. Thus, in extension of Monet's Impressionist credo, motif and viewer are both engulfed in the atmospheric *enveloppe*.

The American painter Lilla Cabot Perry recounted how Monet had said 'he wished he had been born blind and then suddenly had gained his sight so that he could have begun to paint in this way without knowing what the objects were that he saw before him'. This ideal was echoed by Cézanne who, according to Emile Bernard, faced nature determined to forget everything. Significantly, in an age when the fundamental premises of Christianity were being

....
Claude MONET, Grain Stacks,
End of Summer, 1890–91, Paris
Musée d'Orsay. Begun in 1890 but
given the date 1891 when exhibited
with the rest of the Haystacks series at
Durand-Ruel's gallery in May 1891.
....

doubted, both artists felt urged to recreate the world in their own images.

In 1882, after 15 rejections, Cézanne finally had his first, and only, painting accepted by the Salon thanks to the intervention of his juror friend Antoine Guillemet; the work was an as yet unidentified portrait which was badly hung and attracted no notice. In the autumn of that same year Cézanne secluded himself in the south of France, spending less and less time in Paris. This pattern of withdrawal was accelerated by his increasing estrangement from Hortense (whom he nonetheless married in 1886 to legitimize their child), the termination of his friendship with Zola after being ruthlessly characterized in the novel *L'Oeuvre* (published in 1886), and – most important of all – the death of his father in 1886, which ensured Cézanne a greater measure of financial and emotional independence.

The remaining years of Cézanne's life were instead to be wholly dedicated to his self-proclaimed artistic objectives – to 'vivify Poussin through nature', and to 'make of Impressionism something solid and durable, like the art of the museums'. This reconciliation of sensation and structure was at times to appear an almost insuperable task.

Cézanne's landscapes from the later 1880s onwards tend to be divided between contrasting 'open' and 'enclosed' motifs. Dominating the more open, panoramic treatments of landscape is the Mont Sainte-Victoire, a huge limestone eminence, 10 miles (16km) from Aix, which Cézanne painted more than 60 times in oil and watercolour. Views from his brother-in-law's estate at Belleville across the Arc Valley (c.1885–7) and from a specially built studio (c.1901–6) at Chemin des Lauves, in the hills east of Aix, both offered the age-old landscapist's challenge of a spacious, flattish middle distance which extended to the base of the mountain's sculptural mass. In Cézanne's final pantheistic celebrations of the mountain he deliberately allows horizontals to predominate, 'flattening' the composition and making more difficult the task of convincingly receding an

....
Claude MONET, Populars on the
Epte, *1891, Edinburgh, National
Gallery of Scotland. This is one of
several treatments of the same view of
trees, near the artist's home at
Giverny, made in 1891.*
....

....
Paul CÉZANNE, Les Grandes
Baigneuses (The Large Bathers),
*c. 1898–1905, London, National
Gallery.*
....

Paul CÉZANNE, Mont
Sainte Victoire, c.1904–6,
Zurich, Buhrle Foundation.

already flattened middle distance. Yet without disturbing the composition's balance between flatness and solidity, Cézanne achieves exactly this recession by painstakingly constructing the middle ground with a mosaic of horizontal, diagonal and vertical patches of colour, each corresponding to the simple conical, spherical and cylindrical forms which he (and indeed, Poussin) believed were the building-blocks of nature.

Cézanne's use of colour, rather than line, to suggest plastic form can be seen in an even more concentrated vein in his paintings of 'enclosed' forest scenes. Towards the end of his career he turned increasingly to watercolour, and the influence of this technique on his late oil paintings can be seen in the *Grounds of the Château Noir* (1904–6, London, National Gallery). The paint now tends to be thinly applied in diagonally set, rectangular patches of colour which modify each other where they interlock. With minimal use of linear description, these produce formidably solid forms, which at the same time harmonize the surface of the composition.

The levels of exactitude required of this technique were highlighted by a well-known, if perhaps apocryphal, account given by the dealer Ambroise Vollard of the painting of his portrait by Cézanne in 1899 (Paris, Musée du Petit Palais). Vollard sat for no fewer than 115 sessions before Cézanne eventually abandoned the portrait, unfinished. When asked what he thought of the portrait, Cézanne replied 'I am not dissatisfied with the shirtfront'.

But Cézanne's late work is not merely a matter of analytical technique. These paintings also recapture and rechannel the emotional power of his youth, energizing his late still lifes. for example, with an unexpected Baroque opulence and sense of mobility. The latter effect, in anticipation of Cubism, was a result of using slightly different viewpoints for individual elements in the composition.

The varied strands of Cézanne's career seem to have been consciously brought together between 1900 and 1905 in three monumental scenes of female *Bathers* (now in The Barnes Foundation, The National Gallery, London, and The Philadelphia Museum of Art). In Cézanne's *Bathers* (London, National Gallery) are the reformed temptresses of his macabre early works, now harmonized into a composition remarkable, in the words of Matisse, for 'the exceptional sobriety of its relationships'. Combining elements of figure painting, still life, and landscape, the *Bathers* is a calculated piece of picture-making, an

....
Claude MONET, Waterlilies, *after
1916, London, National Gallery.
One of several canvases depicting this
theme found in Monet's studio
following his death.*
....

exercise in arcadian classicism to be placed beside the museum art of Poussin.

Cézanne's *Bathers* and Monet's *Waterlilies* have much in common as final testaments. Both owed their genesis to the imagination and memory, and both were executed on a large scale, entirely in the studio.

Can either of these series, then, have anything in

common with the vibrant, spontaneous works that revolutionized Parisian art decades before? The verdict should come from Camille Pissarro, that most courageous, but self-effacing of the Impressionists, who in November 1895 wrote a letter to his painter son Lucien, in which he recalled that year's Cézanne exhibition at Vollard's gallery in Paris:

I also thought of Cézanne's show in which there are exquisite things, still lifes of irreproachable perfection, others, *much worked on* and yet unfinished, of even greater beauty, landscapes, nudes, and heads that are unfinished but yet grandiose, and so *painted*, so supple . . . Why? Sensation is there! (J. Wechsler, *Cézanne in Perspective*, Prentice Hall, 1975.)

SELECT BIBLIOGRAPHY

The author wishes to acknowledge his debt to many sources and recommends the following bibliography for further reading:

GENERAL

BAUDELAIRE, Charles, *The Painter of Modern Life and Other Essays*, translated by Jonathan Mayne (New York, 1964)

BERNARD, Bruce (ed.), *The Impressionist Revolution* (London, 1986)

BOIME, Albert, *The Academy and French Painting in the Nineteenth Century* (Oxford, 1973)

BRETTELL, R (ed.), *A Day in the Country: Impressionism and the French Landscape* (Los Angeles County Museum of Art, 1984)

CALLEN, Anthea, *Techniques of the Impressionists* (London, 1987)

DENVIR, Bernard (ed.), *The Impressionists at First Hand* (London, 1987)

EITNER, Lorenz, *An Outline of 19th-Century European Painting: From David through Cézanne* (New York, 1987)

HOUSE, John (ed.), *Impressionism: Its Masters, its Precursors, and its Influence in Britain* (Exhibition catalogue, London, Royal Academy, 1974)

MOFFETT, Charles (ed.), *The New Painting: Impressionism 1874–1886* (Exhibition catalogue, Fine Arts Museums of San Francisco, 1986)

NOCHLIN, Linda, *Impressionism and Post-Impressionism 1874–1904: Sources and Documents* (Englewood Cliffs, New Jersey, 1966)

NOCHLIN, Linda, *Realism* (London, 1971)

POOL, Phoebe, *Impressionism* (London, 1967)

REWALD, John, *The History of Impressionism* (New York and London, 4th revised edition 1973)

CÉZANNE

CHAPPUIS, A, *The Drawings of Cézanne, A Catalogue Raisonée* (2 vols, Greenwich, Conn., and London, 1973)

GOWING, L and others, *Cézanne: The Early Years 1859–72* (Exhibition catalogue, London, Royal Academy, 1988)

REWALD, John, *Paul Cézanne, A Biography* (New York, 1968)

REWALD, John, *Paul Cézanne, The Watercolours* (New York, 1983)

RUBIN, W, *Cézanne: The Late Work* (Exhibition catalogue, New York, Metropolitan Museum of Art, 1977)

SCHAPIRO, M, *Paul Cézanne* (New York, 1952)

VENTURI, L, *Cézanne, Son Art et Son Oeuvre* (2 vols, Paris, 1936)

WECHSLER, J (ed.), *Cézanne in Perspective* (Englewood Cliffs, New Jersey, 1975)

DEGAS

ADHEMER, J and CACHIN, F, *Degas, The Complete Etchings, Lithographs and Monotypes* (New York, 1975)

BOGGS, J S, *Portraits by Degas* (Berkeley, 1962)

DUNLOP, I, *Degas* (New York, 1979)

GUERIN, M, *Degas Letters* (Oxford, 1947)

MCMULLEN, R, *Degas, His Life, Times and Work* (Boston, 1984)

MILLARD, C W, *The Sculpture of Edgar Degas* (Princeton, 1976)

GRAND PALAIS *Degas* (Exhibition catalogue, Paris, 1988)

REFF, Theodore, *Degas, The Artist's Mind* (New York, 1976)

REFF, Theodore, *The Notebooks of Edgar Degas* (2 vols, Oxford, 1976)

MANET

CLARK, T J, *The Painting of Modern Life: Paris in the Art of Manet and his Followers* (London, 1985)

COFFIN HANSON, Anne, *Manet and the Modern Tradition* (Yale, 1977)

REFF, T, *Manet and Modern Paris* (Exhibition catalogue, Washington DC, National Gallery, 1982)

REFF, T, *Manet's 'Olympia'* (Allen Lane, 1976)

ROUART, D and WILDENSTEIN, D, *Edouard Manet: Catalogue Raisonnée* (2 vols, Geneva, 1975)

WILSON, Michael, *Manet at Work* (Exhibition catalogue, London, National Gallery, 1983)

MONET

GORDON, R and FORGE, A, *Monet* (New York, 1983)

HAMILTON, G H, *Claude Monet's Paintings of Rouen Cathedral* (London, 1960)

HOUSE, John, *Monet: Nature into Art* (Yale, 1986)

ISAACSON, J, *Monet: Le Déjeuner sur l'Herbe* (New York, 1972)

JOYES, C, *Monet at Giverny* (New York, 1976)

LEVINE, S Z, *Monet and his Critics* (New York, 1976)

ROUART, D and REY, J D, *Monet, Nympheas* (Paris, 1972)

SEIBERLING, G, *Monet's Series* (New York and London, 1981)

SEITZ, W, *Monet* (New York, 1960)

TUCKER, F, *Monet at Argenteuil* (New Haven and London, 1982)

WILDENSTEIN, D, *Claude Monet, Biographie et Catalogue Raisonée* (4 vols, Lausanne, 1974–1985)

WILDENSTEIN, D and others, *Monet's Years at Giverny: Beyond Impressionism* (New York, 1978)

PISSARRO

LLOYD, C, *Pissarro* (New York, 1981)

LLOYD, C and others, *Pissarro* (Exhibition catalogue, London, Hayward Gallery, 1980–81)

REWALD, J, *Camille Pissarro: Letters to his Son Lucien* (New York, 1943)

REWALD, J, *Pissarro* (New York, 1963)

SHIKES, R and HARPER, R, *Pissarro, His Life and Work* (New York, 1980)

VENTURI, L, *Camille Pissarro, Son Art, Son Oeuvre* (2 vols, Paris, 1939)

RENOIR

ANDRE, A and ELDER, M, *L'Atelier de Renoir* (2 vols, Paris, 1931)

DAULTE, F, *Auguste Renoir, Watercolours, Pastels and Drawings in Colour* (London, 1959)

GAUNT, W and ADLER, K, *Renoir* (Oxford, 1982)

HOUSE, J, GOWING, L, DISTEL, A and others, *Renoir* (Exhibition catalogue, Arts Council of Great Britain, 1985)

PACH, W, *Renoir* (New York, 1950)

RENOIR, J, *Renoir, My Father* (New York, 1962)

WHITE, E B, *Renoir* (New York, 1984)

SISLEY

BERN, KUNSTMUSEUM *Alfred Sisley* (Exhibition catalogue, 1958)

COGNIAT, C, *Sisley* (Paris and New York, 1978)

DAULTE, F, *Alfred Sisley, Catalogue de l'Oeuvre Peint* (Lausanne, 1959)

NATHANSON, R, *Alfred Sisley* (Exhibition catalogue, London, 1981)

SHONE, R, *Sisley* (London, 1979)

POST-IMPRESSIONISM AND IMPRESSIONISM ABROAD

BARON, W, *Sickert* (London, 1973)

BROUDE, N, *Seurat in Perspective* (Englewood Cliffs, NJ, 1978)

DORRA, H and REWALD, J, *Seurat, L'Oeuvre Peint, Biographie et Catalogue Raisonée* (Paris, 1959)

GERDTS, W H, *American Impressionism* (New York, 1984)

DE HAUKE, C M, *Seurat et Son Oeuvre* (Paris, 1961)

HERBERT, R L, *Neo-Impressionism* (New York, Guggenheim Museum, 1968)

HOUSE, J, ROSENTHAL, N and others, *Post-Impressionism* (Exhibition catalogue, London, Royal Academy, 1979–80)

LAUGHTON, B, *Philip Wilson Steer* (London, 1971)

RUSSELL, J, *Seurat* (London, 1965)

INDEX